1 MONTH OF
FREE
READING

at
www.ForgottenBooks.com

By purchasing this book you are eligible for one month membership to ForgottenBooks.com, giving you unlimited access to our entire collection of over 1,000,000 titles via our web site and mobile apps.

To claim your free month visit:

www.forgottenbooks.com/free918631

ISBN 978-0-265-97882-5
PIBN 10918631

The Shepherd College Picket

New Vol. XXII   Shepherdstown, W. Va.   Number 4

Catalogue Number

SHEPHERD COLLEGE

State Normal School

Issued July, 1917

Entered at the Postoffice at Shepherdstown as Second Class Mail Matter

MAIN BUILDING

FORTY-FIFTH
ANNUAL CATALOGUE
SHEPHERD COLLEGE
STATE NORMAL SCHOOL
1917-1918

Announcements 1917-1918

ISSUED JULY, 1917

SHEPHERDSTOWN, WEST VIRGINIA

WHEELING NEWS LITHO. CO.
WHEELING, W. VA.

Official Boards

1917

SEPTEMBER

S	M	T	W	T	F	S
						1
2	3	4	5	6	7	8
9	10	11	12	13	14	15
16	17	18	19	20	21	22
23	24	25	26	27	28	29
30						

OCTOBER

S	M	T	W	T	F	S
	1	2	3	4	5	6
7	8	9	10	11	12	13
14	15	16	17	18	19	20
21	22	23	24	25	26	27
28	29	30	31			

NOVEMBER

S	M	T	W	T	F	S
				1	2	3
4	5	6	7	8	9	10
11	12	13	14	15	16	17
18	19	20	21	22	23	24
25	26	27	28	29	30	

DECEMBER

S	M	T	W	T	F	S
						1
2	3	4	5	6	7	8
9	10	11	12	13	14	15
16	17	18	19	20	21	22
23	24	25	26	27	28	29
30	31					

1918

JANUARY

S	M	T	W	T	F	S
		1	2	3	4	5
6	7	8	9	10	11	12
13	14	15	16	17	18	19
20	21	22	23	24	25	26
27	28	29	30	31		

FEBRUARY

S	M	T	W	T	F	S
					1	2
3	4	5	6	7	8	9
10	11	12	13	14	15	16
17	18	19	20	21	22	23
24	25	26	27	28		

MARCH

S	M	T	W	T	F	S
					1	2
3	4	5	6	7	8	9
10	11	12	13	14	15	16
17	18	19	20	21	22	23
24	25	26	27	28	29	30
31						

APRIL

S	M	T	W	T	F	S
	1	2	3	4	5	6
7	8	9	10	11	12	13
14	15	16	17	18	19	20
21	22	23	24	25	26	27
28	29	30				

MAY

S	M	T	W	T	F	S
			1	2	3	4
5	6	7	8	9	10	11
12	13	14	15	16	17	18
19	20	21	22	23	24	25
26	27	28	29	30	31	

JUNE

S	M	T	W	T	F	S
						1
2	3	4	5	6	7	8
9	10	11	12	13	14	15
16	17	18	19	20	21	22
23	24	25	26	27	28	29
30						

JULY

S	M	T	W	T	F	S
	1	2	3	4	5	6
7	8	9	10	11	12	13
14	15	16	17	18	19	20
21	22	23	24	25	26	27
28	29	30	31			

AUGUST

S	M	T	W	T	F	S
				1	2	3
4	5	6	7	8	9	10
11	12	13	14	15	16	17
18	19	20	21	22	23	24
25	26	27	28	29	30	31

SEPTEMBER

S	M	T	W	T	F	S
1	2	3	4	5	6	7
8	9	10	11	12	13	14
15	16	17	16	19	20	21
22	23	24	25	26	27	28
29	30					

OCTOBER

S	M	T	W	T	F	S
		1	2	3	4	5
6	7	8	9	10	11	12
13	14	15	16	17	18	19
20	21	22	23	24	25	26
27	28	29	30	31		

NOVEMBER

S	M	T	W	T	F	S
					1	2
3	4	5	6	7	8	9
10	11	12	13	14	15	16
17	18	19	20	21	22	23
24	25	26	27	28	29	30

DECEMBER

S	M	T	W	T	F	S
1	2	3	4	5	6	7
8	9	10	11	12	13	14
15	16	17	18	19	20	21
22	23	24	25	26	27	28
29	30	31				

RENDERING PATRIOTIC SERVICE ON THE FARM, AND A NUMBER CALLED TO THE COLORS

Commencement Schedule, June 2-8, 1917

Saturday Evening, June 2-----------Recital by Department of Expression

Sunday Evening, June 3------------------------------------Annual Sermon
Dr. J. Edward Harms, Pastor St. John's Lutheran Church,
Hagerstown, Md.

Monday Evening, June 4-----------------Recital by Department of Music

Tuesday Evening, June 5-----------------------------Senior Class Play

Wednesday Evening, June 6-----------------------Inter-Society Contest

Thursday Morning, June 7-----------------Finals in Tennis Tournament

Thursday Afternoon, June 7---
Exhibit of Art, Manual Training and Domestic Science Departments

Thursday Evening, June 7------------------Alumni Reunion and Banquet

Friday Morning, June 8---------------------------Graduating Exercises
Address before the Senior Class by Hon. N. G. Keim of Elkins, member of the Board of Regents. Presentation of diplomas by Hon. M. P. Shawkey, State Superintendent of Schools.

Announcements, 1917-1918

Fall Term opens Tuesday, September 18, 1917.

Fall Term closes Friday, December 21, 1917.

Winter Term opens Wednesday, January 2, 1918

Winter Term closes Thursday, March 21, 1918

Spring Term opens Tuesday, March 26, 1918

Spring Term closes Tuesday, June 11, 1918

Summer Term opens Tuesday, June 11, 1918.

Faculty

Professional Subjects
THOS. C. MILLER, Principal
Fairmont State Normal School; Adrian College

Modern Languages, Algebra
WALTER M. DUKE, First Assistant
Graduate Shepherd College State Normal School; A.B., West Virginia
University; Graduate Student Columbia University

History, Economics, Civics
MABEL HENSHAW-GARDINER
M.P.L., New Windsor College; A.B., West Virginia University

English
ELLA MAY TURNER
Graduate Shepherd College State Normal School; A.M., West Virginia
University; Graduate Student Cornell University

Latin and English
LOUISE J. SMITH
Graduate High School, Washington, D. C.; A.B., George Washington
University

Physics, Chemistry, Geometry
A. D. KENAMOND
Graduate West Liberty Normal; A.B., West Virginia University; Graduate Student West Virginia University and University of Chicago

Agriculture, Biology, Geography
J. D. MULDOON
Graduate West Liberty Normal; A.B., West Virginia University

Education and Supervisor Training
S. O. BOND
Graduate Salem College; A.B., West Virginia University; A.M., Columbia
University; Graduate Student Columbia University toward Ph.D.

Art
ADDIE R. IRELAND

Graduate Morgantown High School; Graduate Art Department, West Virginia University; Student, Art Students' League, New York City; Student Arts and Technology, University of Chicago

Home Economics
*CATHERINE COWSILL

Graduate Central High School, Washington, D. C., and National School of Domestic Art and Science; Student Columbia University

Manual Training and Athletics
R. O. McBRIEN

University of Nebraska, Maryland Agricultural College

Music
MAGGIE LILLIAN MERRELLS

Graduate Buckhannon High School; Graduate West Virginia Wesleyan Conservatory of Music; Teachers' Training Course and Graduate Work West Virginia Wesleyan College

Commercial Subjects
ETTA O. WILLIAMS

Graduate Washington County High School and Columbia Business College, Hagerstown, Md.; Student Columbia University

Expression
MARY E. GIBSON
Teachers in Graded School

Floyd B. Mathias (Class of 1916) _____Principal and Eighth Grade

Kirkland McKee (Class of 1916) _____Seventh Grade

Ella M. Kelsey (Class of 1874) _____Sixth Grade

Julia Hill_____Fifth Grade

Louise Righstine (Class of 1909) _____Fourth Grade

Alice Banks (Class of 1906) _____Third Grade

Bessie Licklider (Class of 1897) _____Second Class

Ruth Taylor (Class of 1912) _____First Grade

---

*On leave of absence, fall 1916, when her place was taken by Katrina Baumgardner of the National School of Domestic Science and Domestic Art.

Shepherd College State Normal School

HISTORY

Shepherd College dates its founding as a State Normal School to an Act of the Legislature of West Virginia, passed February 27, 1872; but it had its incipiency in a classical and scientific school styled "Shepherd College," certificate of incorporation of which is on record at Charleston, January 12, 1872. As an inducement to secure a Normal School here the trustees of this private school offered its building to the State free of charge for use as a State Normal School, which offer was promptly accepted, and work under State control began in September, 1873.

LOCATION

The location of the school is most ideal. Situated in the charming old town of Shepherdstown, nestled on the cliffy crags of the beautiful and historic Potomac which sweeps in graceful curves across the Shenandoah Valley at this point, remarkably free from all insidious fevers and diseases, with a wholesome social and moral atmosphere, an educated and cultured community, comparatively easy of access, it offers unsurpassed attractions and advantages to the earnest student.

The school is located on scenic and historic ground. To the east loom up the fine wooded sides of the Blue Ridge, and to the west those of the North Mountain. The Potomac river flows past the town and affords fine boating and fishing, while on its northern bank is the old historic Chesapeake and Ohio Canal which, with its canal boats drawn by mules, forms even in this day of railroads an important means of transportation. To the south and north spreads out the broad, beautiful and historic valley of Virginia. Three miles to the north is Sharpsburg and the battlefield of Antietam with its fine monuments and National Cemetery, while some seventy miles to the south is the famous Luray Cavern. The same distance to the east is Washington, the nation's capital. All of these things cannot fail to leave their permanent impress on the mind of the observant student.

HOW TO REACH SHEPHERDSTOWN

Shepherdstown is on the Norfolk and Western Railroad, which connects with the main line of the Baltimore and Ohio Railroad at Shenan-

GRADUATING CLASS, 1917

doah Junction, six miles to the south; or with the Western Maryland Railroad at Hagerstown, Md., eighteen miles to the north.

Students who live on or near the Baltimore and Ohio lines will come via that road to Shenandoah Junction, from which point they may come via the N. & W. to Shepherdstown. The connections between these roads are at times so poor that many who come by that route find it more convenient to drive from Shenandoah Junction to Shepherdstown, it being a comparatively inexpensive drive over six miles of the Shenandoah Valley. Conveyances may be secured at Shenandoah Junction or ordered from Shepherdstown in advance.

Those who live on or near the Western Maryland lines will purchase tickets to Hagerstown, the connections at this point being most excellent at this time, students being able to reach Shepherdstown before night of the same day of starting from points as far distant as Elkins. This is decidedly the best route for all to whom it is accessible.

Students from Pendleton, Grant and Hardy counties, and neighboring districts, can take the Hampshire Southern road at Petersburg and Moorefield and intermediate points and make connections at Romney and Green Spring with trains east on the Baltimore and Ohio road.

As will appear from the above, Shepherdstown is not an inaccessible place, as is sometimes supposed by those who live in the Trans-Alleghany portion of the State. It can be reached in a single day from all railroad points in a large majority of all the counties of West Virginia.

TRANSPORTATION FACILITIES

The latest available time tables show the following schedules on the railroads:

N. & W. South

No. 27—Hagerstown, 5 :00 P. M.; Shepherdstown, 5 :33 P. M.
No. 13—Hagerstown, 8 :00 A. M.; Shepherdstown, 8 :30 A. M.

N. & W. North

No. 14—Berryville, 7 :04 P. M.; Shenandoah Junction, 7 :50 P. M.; Shepherdstown, 8 :04 P. M.
No. 28—Berryville, 8 :32 A. M.; Shenandoah Junction, 9 :25 A. M.; Shepherdstown, 9 :35 A. M.

Western Maryland East

No. 10—Elkins, 7 :40 A. M.; W. Va. Central Junction, 11 :44 A. M.; Cumberland, 1 :40 P. M.; Hagerstown, 4 :00 P. M.

B. & O. East

No. 32—Cumberland, 6:15 A. M.; Martinsburg, 8:52 A. M.; Shenandoah Junction, 9:21 A. M.

No. 6—Terra Alta, 9:45 A. M.; Cumberland, 12:45 P. M.; Green Spring, 1:06 P. M.; Martinsburg, 2:43 P. M.; Shenandoah Junction, 3:03 P. M. (special stop).

No. 34—Cumberland, 3:15 P. M.; Green Spring, 3:44 P. M; Shenandoah Junction, 6:28 P. M.

Hampshire Southern North

No. 66—Petersburg, 8:00 A. M.; Romney, 11:30 A. M.; Green Spring, 12:25 P. M.

CONDITIONS OF ADMISSION

An age, an educational and a moral qualification are required for admission to this school. Students cannot be admitted under fourteen years of age. A fair knowledge of the common school branches is a pre-requisite to entrance. Only students of good moral character will be admitted. Beginning September, 1920, all except mature students entering for the spring term must have completed one year of high school work.

CREDIT FOR WORK DONE ELSEWHERE

Credit will be given students for satisfactory work done in other Normal Schools of the State, and also for work completed in such high schools, academies, seminaries, etc., as will seem, in the estimation of the principal, to deserve accredited standing. Before receiving such credit students must present a written statement from such schools, signed by the principal or superintendent, setting forth in detail the work satisfactorily completed there.

These credits should be brought and presented by the student at the time of entrance to Principal Thos. C. Miller, to S. O. Bond or to A. D. Kenamond, who acts as secretary to the committee of which the first named two are members.

Credits may also be allowed on subjects passed on the uniform Examination, provided the certificate shows a high grade. Usually a No. 1 Certificate will practically satisfy the work of the first year. The scheme of crediting from the certificate toward Short Course work appears under the outline of that course.

HOW TO ENROLL

The student, upon arrival, should come to the Principal's office, fill out a card enrolling and pay the fees. If any work has been done elsewhere, credits should be presented to the above named committee on entrance, who will indicate in a general way the classification of the student. Freshmen will present themselves to Miss Smith, Sophomores to Mrs. Gardiner, Junior Secondary to Mr. Muldoon, Senior Secondary and Short Course to Mr. Kenamond, Junior Normal to Mr. Duke and Senior Normal students to Mr. Bond. These teachers will be found in their regular classrooms and will assist the student in making out programs of work.

AMOUNT OF WORK TAKEN

According to a uniform ruling for all the normal schools of the State, five units is the maximum allowed in the secondary or high school course. Four and a half units, or thirty-six hours for the year, is the maximum in the normal course. Four subjects will usually prove sufficient for the average student.

TUITION

Tuition is free to all West Virginia students, except that all students are required to pay an incidental fee of two dollars per term and an athletic fee of one dollar per term. This applies to both the Secondary and Normal departments, but does not apply to the departments of Music and Elocution, in which reasonable tuition charges are made. Students from outside the State, and others not entitled to receive instruction in this school by reason of their age, will be required to pay additional tuition at the rate of four dollars per term of twelve to fourteen weeks.

EXPENSES

Few schools of similar grade in this State or elsewhere can offer students so reasonable an expense account as can Shepherd College Normal. No tuition is charged students from this State pursuing any of the regular courses of studies. No fees are exacted except an incidental fee of $2.00 per term and an athletic fee of $1.00 per term, both payable in advance. Subjoined is a table which exhibits a careful estimate of a student's minimum and maximum necessary expenses for a year of thirty-eight weeks:

Board and room	$125.00 to	$165.00
Books and stationery	9.00 to	18.00
Laundry	10.00 to	20.00
Enrollment fees	6.00 to	6.00
Athletic fees	3.00 to	3.00
Tuition fees	0.00 to	12.00
Student organizations	1.00 to	4.00
	$154.00 to	$228.00

To this should be added traveling and incidental expenses, which will vary with the distance traveled in coming to the school, and with the personal habits and inclinations of the student.

STUDENT LOAN FUND

A few years ago a student loan fund amounting to about $150 was contributed by alumni of the school, and several worthy young people have already been aided. This year the graduating class has invested $100 in a liberty bond and the Faculty $50, both contributing thus to the loan fund. It is hoped that the number and size of contributions will continue to increase.

The fund is in charge of Principal Thos. C. Miller, a member of the Faculty who will usually be an alumnus of the school and a local alumnus. Applications for loans from the fund should be made to the principal of the school.

BOOKS

Students will do well to bring with them any books they may have, but should not purchase new books until they have enrolled and been assigned to their studies.

Students of the more advanced classes frequently have second-hand books for sale at from three-fifths to four-fifths of the original cost.

New books may be secured from Mr. Duke at cost.

BOARDING

So far as the accommodations will allow, girls without friends or relatives in town room and board in the dormitory. All desiring a room should write the Principal of the school early. The rate has been fixed at $3.25 per week.

Many of the best homes in the town accommodate student roomers and boarders. Girls who fail to secure places in the dormitory take advantage of the privileges, and all boys find accommodations with private families, where they seem to be well satisfied with their treatment.

The Principal has jurisdiction over these boarding places, and persons who keep student boarders are required to enforce any regulation in reference to the conduct of students in their homes as he may from time to time find necessary to prescribe.

Students are assisted in finding suitable boarding places by the Principal and by the Y. W. C. A. and Y. M. C. A. of the school.

JUNIOR CLASSES

RELIGIOUS INFLUENCES

It is not to be supposed because this is a State school and in no way connected with any religious denomination or sect that it encourages any the less character-building and religious living. On the contrary, it is often found that the moral and religious atmosphere that pervades State schools such as this is in every way as wholesome and as conducive to upright Christian living as that of schools which are under the denomination of some religious sect.

Students are expected to attend at least one service each Sunday in the church of their choice. Shepherdstown has most excellent advantages in this regard, there being no fewer than seven churches having regular services, presided over by a clergy of unusual ability for so small a town. Students are welcomed to their services by both pastors and congregations and find here a pleasant church home. Many of the students are active workers in the Sunday schools and churches, as are also members of the faculty, most of whom are active members.

SOCIAL DIVERSIONS

Social diversions of a pleasing and cultural character are not lacking here. Receptions are given each year by the faculty to the students, who, in turn, give receptions to the faculty. The various organizations also receive at stated intervals. Al of these functions are given under proper supervision and they do much toward bringing about that cordial and sympathetic relationship between faculty and students that is so characteristic of this school.

Equipment

BUILDINGS

The school has now three large and commodious buildings in which to carry on its work. The oldest of the three is the original Shepherd College. This was transferred by perpetual lease to the Board of Trustees of Shepherd College by Shepherd Brooks, Esq., of Boston. This Board, which is a self-perpetuating body, put the building at the State's disposal for normal school purposes at the school's first founding; and it was the sole home of the school continuously until 1897, when the school occupied a new building erected just north of the College, which was destroyed by fire in the spring of 1901. The "College" is now used as a music hall and is also headquarters for the literary societies. It contains six commodious rooms.

Adjoining the above is Shepherd College Hall, which was erected in 1889 by the citizens of Shepherdstown and was put at the disposal of the school. It was used until recently for commencement exercises, lectures, receptions, etc., and was the place for holding chapel services. It is now headquarters for the Department of Domestic Science and Domestic Art. In a basement room of this building the machinery of the Manual Training Department is operated.

The new Shepherd College building was completed and first occupied in the spring of 1904. It is thoroughly modern and well appointed. The basement contains a large gymnasium, lavatories, toilet rooms, a manual training shop and laboratories for biology and agriculture. The first floor contains the principal's office, general office, study hall, library, cloak rooms and six commodious class rooms. On the second floor are found a fine auditorium, with a seating capacity of about seven hundred, five class rooms, cloak rooms, etc. This building, as also the other, is heated by hot water. The boiler-house is a short distance from the main structure. Water for lavatory and other uses is pumped from a cistern to all parts of the building. Water for drinking purposes is supplied from a good well. The building is lighted by electricity. The grounds have been beautified by the planting of trees, shrubbery and flowers.

LABORATORIES

The Biology and Agricultural Laboratories occupy two of the rooms recently equipped to meet increasing needs growing out of our enriched curriculum. They are plumbed for water and furnished with biological tables accommodating twenty-four students at one time. Each table is supplied with a student's dissecting microscope, and each group of eight students has access to a splendid Spencer microscope magnifying above 400 diameters. A Babcock tester, germinating boxes, seed testers, a De-Laval separator loaned by the manufacturer, insect nets and mounts, and numerous other pieces of apparatus are at hand. An excellent collection of zoological specimens has been made and a school garden on the grounds offers opportunity for illustrative work.

The Chemistry Laboratory has accommodations for sixteen students at one time, and is equipped with all necessary chemicals and apparatus for standard work in first year chemistry. Alcohol lamps, gasoline burners and an electric hot plate are used for heating, while the faucets supply soft water.

The Physics Laboratory is well supplied with demonstration apparatus. There are three physics tables and three complete sets of apparatus for individual experiments.

The Domestic Science Department is fitted up with a large steel range, tables for twenty-four students, and all necessary culinary apparatus for individual and group work. For Domestic Art three Singer sewing machines and several cutting tables are provided.

The Manual Training Department is supplied with a band saw and a hand jointer, both operated by electric motor. Twenty students may work at one time at the tables, which are provided with the usual tools.

Numerous geological specimens, maps, tellurians and charts meet the needs of Geography for illustrative teaching. A mounted skeleton, plaster casts and models are valuable aids to the Physiology classes.

LIBRARY

The library occupies a handsome and exceptionally well-lighted room adjoining the study hall. It is open from 8 A. M. until 4:30 P. M. every school day, from 6 to 8 at night, from 10 to 12 and from 2 to 4 on Saturday. Books may be taken out and kept not exceeding two weeks. It contains over 4,000 well-selected bound volumes and several hundred pamphlets, periodicals and magazines. The library is used also as a reading room, and on the tables and racks may be found about seventy of the best current magazines, periodicals and newspapers. This equipment is being very rapidly added to, important additions being made to it each year.

THE GYMNASIUM

In a climate like ours, where during much of the year the weather is unfit for out of door sports, it is essential that schools have gymnasiums of dimensions adequate to admit of various indoor games and exercises, and equipped with all needed appliances for the development of the physi-

cal man. Shepherd College possesses such a gymnasium. It occupies a
large part of the basement of the new building, and is equipped with first-
class gymnasium appliances, making it one of the best gymnasiums in this
section of the country.

THE DORMITORY

Just two squares from the main building a three-story Colonial dormitory has been erected during the past year. It is modern in every detail and offers advantages that have been demanded by our patrons for
some years. The dining room with a capacity of one hundred or more,
laundry, kitchen, serving room and the heater room are on the first floor.
On the second floor are a large reception room, a rest room, library and
nine bed rooms 15x12. Each bed room contains two closets with shelves
and lavatory with hot and cold water. Bath rooms and lavatories are
found at each end of the corridor. The third floor contains thirteen bed
rooms, a hall and lavatories. The east, north and south sides have porches.

GROUNDS

The grounds about the various buildings are remarked for their
beauty, and careful attention is given to keep them beautiful. Magnificent
shade trees, fruit trees in bearing, flower gardens and growing vegetables
of many varieties and the "Town Run" flowing through a corner of one
of the plats all go to make up a delightful composite whole. Two tennis
courts and a baseball park appeal to many.

FRESHMAN CLASS

Student Organizations

LITERARY SOCIETIES

There are two flourishing literary societies in the school—the Ciceronian and the Parthenian. They are volunteer organizations, and hold meetings every Friday afternoon during the school year. They are, of course, presided over by students of the school, which affords all a most excellent opportunity of acquainting themselves with parliamentary usage and custom. Primarily, they are for the purpose of developing and nurturing, in the most practical way, a taste for and the ability to do literary work of merit. This they are accomplishing in a very satisfactory manner, as is attested by the success of our students and graduates in literary contests. The annual Inter-Society Contest is doing much to stimulate the work of the societies.

Following are the names of the contestants for this year's Inter-Society Contest held on the evening of June 6:

Parthenian		Ciceronian
George Hartzell	Debaters	H. L. Snyder, Jr.
Hobart Roby	Orators	Lamont Pyles
Agnes Bell	Declaimers	Ethel Scott
Margaret Appel	Essayists	Margaret I. Lindsay

L'EXTEMPO

L'Extempo is an extemporaneous debating society, organized a few years ago by the young men of this institution. Meetings are held every Friday night in Parthenian Hall, and on the third Friday night of each month public meetings are held to which all visitors are welcome. Only members may attend and participate in other meetings. At these meetings all debates are extemporaneous and each member is expected to take part in the discussions. The training that comes to each student who identifies himself with this organization consists not only in the self-confidence, ready expression and skill in debating, but also in the tact and discipline of parliamentary law.

WILLARD CLUB

For some time the need had been felt for an organization which would give the girls of Shepherd College special practice in debating. To meet this demand twenty student girls met March 28, 1913, and organized the Willard Club, the purpose of which is to give training in debate and public speaking. All girls in Shepherd College are eligible. Meetings are held every Friday night in Ciceronian Hall. On the second Friday night of each month the meeting is open to the public and all visitors are welcome. Only members may be present at other meetings. The aims of the club are to promote interest and to encourage ready and logical discussions on questions of general importance. This part of the girls' education has been so universally neglected that such an organization cannot fail to accomplish great good.

THE ENGLISH CLUB

The English Club was organized during the Winter Term of 1910, and held its first meeting April 1, 1910. The aims of the club are to encourage efforts toward acquiring greater proficiency in English, and to promote good fellowship among the students. Any student having had four courses in English in Shepherd College, with an average of 90 per cent or above, and with no less than 85 per cent on any one term, is eligible. The regular meeting night of the club is the first Friday night of each month during the school year.

Y. M. C. A.

This organization has been one of the most important factors of the school for several years. At present the society consists of some thirty young men. The aim of the Y. M. C. A. is to furnish that influence which will take the place of previous lack of spiritual training or to emphasize what has already been taught; to train young men for Christian leadership; to inculcate a broad fellowship amongst the students; in a word, to aid the school in its chief aim—the making of real men and women.

Y. W. C. A.

A branch of the Young Women's Christian Association was established in this school in 1903. This organization has forty-eight members. It stands for a good influence in the school, its chief aim is to promote moral culture and the social side of life. It now occupies an attractive room in the old building, which we ourselves have furnished. Committees have been appointed to go to all trains to receive new girl students and to help them to secure boarding places. Therefore, if any girl who is thinking of attending school here will kindly notify the president of this association, she will receive immediate and courteous attention as soon as she arrives in Shepherdstown.

SHEPHERD COLLEGE ATHLETIC ASSOCIATION

The student body of the school is organized as an athletic association under a constitution sanctioned by the faculty. This association meets early in the fall term and elects a board of directors which assumes general control of all athletics in the school. This board consists of a representative from each regularly organized class in school, a treasurer from the faculty and a general manager of athletic teams, the latter member of the board being appointed by the principal of the school. Three managers for each branch of athletics are selected by the student body and from each group of managers a chief manager is chosen by the board of directors. This student manager then arranges the schedule for his team, selects referee or umpire, arranges transportation and hotel accommodations for his team or the visiting team, and acts as custodian of all property or equipment used by his team. The position of student manager is a highly responsible one and requires and develops executive ability. It is the privilege and duty of the faculty manager to inspect all correspondence sent out by the student manager and to approve or reject any or all contracts for inter-scholastic contests.

Any member of an athletic team representing the school must maintain a satisfactory standing in at least three regular subjects and in deportment up to and including the week before the game. No manager is permitted to schedule with a team that does not agree to a like standard, and any contract is void when a visiting team fails to present, before the beginning of the game, a list of its eligible players bearing the signature of the principal of the school it represents.

Every student in school is a member of this association by virtue of a fee of one dollar paid at the time of enrollment each term. In return for this fee the student has free use of athletic equipment and free admission to all games held under the auspices of the association.

Tennis, basketball and baseball are the forms of athletics regularly supported.

SHEPHERD COLLEGE ORCHESTRA

Several members of the school, in conjunction with citizens of the town, form this musical organization. Much of the music for entertainments during the year and for commencement is furnished by the orchestra. The school furnishes most of the instruments and instruction is free, and in other ways the school encourages this worthy organization.

Student Publications

THE SHEPHERD COLLEGE PICKET

The Shepherd College Picket is a wide-awake school paper edited by the students of the school with the approval of the faculty. It is published each month during the school year—ten numbers. Its motto is "To interest all in our affairs" and to show what kind of work is being done at Shepherd College. It affords much excellent literary work for the students who belong to the staff of editors or write for its columns. This sprightly school paper has reached its twenty-second year. The first issue was given to the public Thursday, January 30, 1896. Since then the publication has been much improved and is increasing in usefulness. The Picket management takes this means to thank friends, alumni, students and business men whose liberal support in various ways has made its existence possible in the past, and hopes that such favors will be extended in the future.

THE COHONGOROOTA

The Cohongoroota, which made its first appearance in June, 1910, is the College Annual. This interesting publication is issued annually by the Junior class under the supervision of the faculty. The Cohongoroota, or River of the Wild Goose, was the name applied by the Indians to the upper Potomac on whose rocky cliffs the village of Shepherdstown nestles, and where today one of the State's leading educational institutions is located. It was a happy thought, this blending of old association with the new, that enabled the students to select this name as the title of the publication which is so thoroughly representative of all that pertains to their school life. Not only is this volume a medium through which all the school activities find expression, but its stories breathe an inspiration, and its drawings and pictures of school friends and associates will bring back reminiscences that will linger long after the student has said farewell to his Alma Mater. It has also an educational value in that it affords an opportunity for the development of business ability and artistic and literary skill of those students who take part in its publication.

This latter publication has been suspended during the past two years, but it is hoped that the cost will not long continue to be prohibitive.

GIRLS' DORMITORY

Courses of Study

SECONDARY COURSE
FRESHMAN SECONARDY

Fall	Winter	Spring
Required 4		
English 1*	English 2*	English 3*
Algebra 1	Algebra 2	Algebra 3
Biology 1	Biology 2	Biology 3
Art and Music	Art and Music	Art and Music

SOPHOMORE SECONDARY

Fall	Winter	Spring
Required 3		
Rhetoric 1	Rhetoric 2	Rhetoric 3
Geometry 1	Geometry 2	Geometry 3
Latin 1	Latin 2	Latin 3
*Elective 1**		
Ancient History	Mediaeval History	Mythology
Physical Geography	Commercial Geography	Industrial Geography
Typewriting	Business Arithmetic	Bookkeeping

JUNIOR SECONDARY

Fall	Winter	Spring
Required 3		
American Literature 1	American Literature 2	American Literature 3
Modern History 1	Modern History 2	English History
Latin 4	Latin 5	Latin 6
Elective 1		
Physics 1	Physics 2	Physics 3
French or German 1	French or German 2	French or German 3
Solid Geometry	Algebra 4	Trigonometry

SENIOR SECONDARY

Fall	Winter	Spring
Required 3		
English Literature 1	English Literature 2	English Literature 3
American History*	Civics*	West Virginia History*
Chemistry 1	Chemistry 2	Chemistry 3
Elective 1		
Latin, French or German	Latin, French or German	Latin, French or German
Home Economics or	Home Economics or	Home Economics or
Manual Training	Manual Training	Manual Training
Agriculture 1*	Agriculture 2	Agriculture 3

Students must follow as nearly as possible the above order of taking up subjects for study, and should not elect more than one year ahead or back of classification.

Subjects marked * may be credited from a teacher's certificate showing a high grade.

NORMAL COURSE

JUNIOR NORMAL

Fall	Winter	Spring
Required 4		
Agriculture 1*	Agriculture 2	Agriculture 3
Manual Training or	Manual Training or	Manual Training or
Home Economics	Home Economics	Home Economics
How to Study	Pedagogy	Rural Education or
		School Management
Psychology	Training in Art	Hygiene and Sanitation*

SENIOR NORMAL

Fall	Winter	Spring
Required 4		
Methods and Training	Methods and Training	Methods and Training
Public School Music	Public School Music	Expression
Observation	Practice Teaching	Practice Teaching
History of Education	Social Education	School Administration
Elective 1		
Economics	Sociology	Ethics
Nature Study	Child Study	Rural Sociology
Educational Measure-	Bible History	Library Science
ments		
Advanced Rhetoric	Method in English	Literature in the Grades

The Normal Course may be taken up on completion of a four-year course in a high school or of the Secondary Course previousy outlined.

If agriculture and manual training or home economics have been pursued in high school, either academic or professional subjects may be taken in their stead.

The minimum observation and practice required for graduation shall be ninety recitation periods. Approximately sixty of the ninety shall be spent in practice and thirty in observation.

Public school music is required two periods a week during the fall and winter term.

Subjects marked * may be credited from a teacher's certificate showing a high grade.

SHORT COURSE FOR TEACHERS

Required

English, 108 weeks; English and Modern European History, 36 weeks; American History and Civics, 36 weeks; Elementary Science, 36 weeks; Agriculture, 36 weeks; Manual Training (for boys), 36 weeks; Home Economics (for girls), 36 weeks; Drawing and Music, 36 weeks; Rural

Sociology, 12 weeks; Physical and Commercial Geography, 12 weeks; Applied Arithmetic and Accounting, 12 weeks. A total of ten units.

Elective

Three and a half units to be elected from the following: English, 36 weeks; Botany, 36 weeks; Chemistry, 36 weeks; Physics, 18 weeks; Algebra, 36 weeks; Geometry, 36 weeks; Horticulture, 12 weeks; School Gardening, 12 weeks; Poultry Raising, 12 weeks.

Only the last two years of the course are here outlined by terms, since it is expected that the student applying for the course has already completed two years of high school work either in a local high school or in this school, or has taught on a second grade teacher's certificate.

A teacher's certificate may be used to satisfy some of the requirements in subjects. General rules for crediting follow. Two credits or 24 weeks will be given for each of the following subjects, if the student has made as much as 80% on the subject for a certificate in a Uniform Examination in this State, viz., grammar, reading, history, arithmetic, theory and art, agriculture and geography; and a credit of one course or 12 weeks will be allowed in the same way for spelling, penmanship, bookkeeping, general history, civil government, state history and physiology. Maximum credit, 162 weeks.

A credit of 9 weeks on a subject will be allowed for each successful term of school taught, but not more than 72 weeks can be thus allowed. Those expecting to ask for credit for teaching should be prepared to give evidence that the teaching was successful.

JUNIOR

Fall	Winter	Spring
American Literature 1	American Literature 2	American Literature 3
Agriculture 1	Agriculture 2	Agriculture 3
Modern History 1	Modern History 2	English History
Home Economics or Manual Training	Home Economics or Manual Training	Home Economics or Manual Training
Music	Art 1	Art 2

SENIOR

Fall	Winter	Spring
Methods and training	Methods and training	Methods and Training
Principles of Teaching	Child Study	Hygiene and Sanitation
Rural Sociology	Observation and Practice	Rural Education or School Management
American History	Civics	West Virginia History

EXPLANATION OF TERMS

A *unit* consists of one subject for at least five periods per week for thirty-six weeks in secondary or high school course; and four hours per week in work of college grade.

A *credit* consists of one-third of a unit.

An *hour* consists of one hour recitation per week for eighteen weeks. Two laboratory or shop periods per week equal one hour's work.

Program means the daily scheme of work.

NORMAL DIPLOMA

To receive the Normal Diploma the student must complete the Normal Course of study outlined elsewhere and must have an average of 80 per cent on the work pursued. Every Normal graduate is entitled to a number one teacher's certificate, good to teach in any school in the State.

ACADEMIC DIPLOMA

The old academic courses are now grouped under the title, Secondary Course. Strictly speaking, no academic diploma is now issued by the State Board of Regents, but instead a "Certificate of Proficiency," in the exact form of the old academic diploma which it supersedes, is given the gradu-. ate from the Secondary Course. This "certificate" specifies that its holder has completed the Secondary Course of study and will, in most cases, insure its holder ready admission to the best colleges and universities of the land. It stands for a degree of culture and mental discipline not to be despised.

SHORT COURSE DIPLOMA

This diploma makes the student eligible to receive a first grade elementary certificate good for three years and renewable under certain conditions for another period of three years.

TEACHERS' REVIEW COURSES

Shepherd College has had, during every spring term for some years, a so-called teachers' training and review course. This is designed especially to afford all who have already taught school, or who expect to try the teachers' examinations with a view to entering on the teachers' calling, an opportunity to gain a more thorough knowledge of the subjects upon which they must pass examination for their certificates and which they have to teach in their school rooms. All the common school branches are reviewed with such thoroughness that a term's recitations in any one branch will permit. It is easily seen that where a student has had a good

Y. W. C. A. AND Y. M. C. A.

common school training he can get, in most subjects pursued for one term here, so thorough a grounding that he need not fear the uniform examination in those subjects; on the other hand, if he lacks the preliminary training, he may not be able to put himself square with the examination by one term's work here. We have been gratified to note that most of our teachers' training students have been able to secure good certificates. That they have been benefited permanently in their education and in their outlook upon life goes without saying. Even a term's contact with an institution of this kind leaves an impress that is lasting, and, we believe, beneficial.

SUMMER SCHOOL

A summer school for teachers and those expecting to teach was first instituted here during the summer of 1907. The experiment proved so successful that a similar school was again instituted during the summer of 1908, and this year's summer school opened on June 11.

In addition to the mere sanction of the Board of Regents, the summer school is now backed by a special board resolution, empowering it to offer credit work. This has had the effect of establishing it on a firm and—it may safely be predicted—permanent basis. Common school branches and regular credit courses are offered in sufficient number to meet the demands of those who attend.

With our excellent equipment, and with the school atmosphere pervading these halls, we are enabled to offer teachers and prospective teachers unusual advantages in the way of preparing them for the teachers' examinations and for the work of the school room.

Definite announcement of the summer school for 1918 will be made later. It will open immediately following the close of the spring term.

CORRESPONDENCE STUDY

During the past year this school offered several courses by correspondence. This is a method by which students knowing how to study may do some work toward graduation while out of school. The scheme is devised to encourage worthy students only and does not contemplate the mere reading up of a subject to take the chances on an examination. Definite suggestions, directions and questions are worked out in typewritten form and mailed to the student a lesson at a time. The teacher requires written reports on each lesson. One course will usually require the spare time of a teacher, or other person actively engaged, for a period of three months. The following courses have been offered: English history and mediaeval history by Mrs. Gardiner; algebra by Mr. Duke; rhetoric and American literature by Miss Turner; rural education, child study and history of education by Mr. Kenamond. As the time of the faculty permits new courses will be outlined.

The fee for a correspondence course is the same as the regular term enrollment.

EXTENSION SERVICE

Members of the faculty are available for addresses or for instruction of extension classes in eastern pan-handle centers. The cost of transportation should be provided by the community asking for the service. The district institute, community rally and commencement occasion furnish opportunity for Shepherd College to become acquainted with the communities she is intended to serve and also for these communities to become better acquainted with their school through these representatives.

Outline of Work by Departments

ART

Miss Ireland

"I believe in art for the people, of the people and by the people. * * * * I believe that the principles of art can be intelligently presented to the understanding of the ordinary individual so that he may see their application to the affairs of his occupation, his business, his profession and his home."—Bonnie Snow.

Taste to be of use must pervade all classes. Until good things are within the reach of all, and recognized by the majority, it is vain to hope for excellence in any country. It would be well if we realized these facts, for just now in our State there is promise of important industrial developments, and if we would hold a foremost place those engaged in the industrial arts will need a more thorough education than is provided at the present time. Art and industry must go hand in hand, and we must recognize the value of art as a national asset and provide for it organized and persistent support.

Art I.—Introductory art for beginners. A general introductory course for beginners, covering the work usually done in the grammar grades, and designed to prepare them for illustrative drawing in the sciences. It includes freehand perspective, plant, animal and figure drawing in pen and pencil outline, mass and color, also construction and constructive drawing.

Credit—One-third unit.

Art II.—Pictoral representation, perspective drawing, figure and animal.

Credit—One-third unit.

Art III.—Training in art for elementary schools, popularly known as Arts and Crafts. Art I and II pre-requisite. The relation of art to the school, home and community life. This course is designed to meet the needs of the grade teacher in the town and rural schools. It is based on the course of study adopted by the state, and a thorough explanation and interpretation of these books will be given. It will include:

(*a*)—Representation. For primary grades—plant life, landscape, figure and animal drawing, illustrative drawing for stories, special seasons and days, history, etc., objects without perspective in mass and outline. For grammar grades—pose, object drawing in perspective, accented line, flat tone, shading, composition of groups and landscape.

(*b*)—Construction. For primary grades—paper and cardboard construction, mat weaving, clay modeling, basketry and the playhouse. For grammar grades—basketry, bookbinding, stenciling, block printing.

(*c*)—Design—an introductory course in the principles of design. For primary grades—line harmony, spacing, proportion, arrangement, matching of color, with direct application to construction work. For grammar grades—scales of light and dark, massing in two or three values, color theory, studies in repetition, subordination, symmetry, lettering, application to construction, initials, page ornament, posters.

Special study is given to the decoration of the school room and grounds, appropriate pictures for the grades, the teacher's dress.

Credit—One-third unit, or two and one-half hours.

Art IV.—Commercial Art. To be applied to posters and school publications. This course will include lettering and the cartoon, color harmony and a study of the principles of unity, balance and harmony as applied to the book.

Mediums used are pencil, color, pen and ink.

Art V.—Applied Design. The topics are principles of design, rhythm, balance and harmony as applied to the crafts; paper and cardboard construction; leather and china.

Art VI.—Principles of Design and its Application to the Home. The course consists of talks, class discussions and some drawing. A study of color in relation to the house and dress. Furniture as regards utility, construction, period styles. Framing and hanging pictures.

Art VII.—Art Interpretation. The purpose of this course is to acquaint pupils with the masterpieces of architecture, sculpture and paintings that are recognized by competent judges and to interest them in American art. Description, meaning and history of pictures are features, but the aim is the study of art form. Art history by periods will be considered with a special study of the art of Washington, D. C.

COMMERCIAL WORK

Miss Williams

Work in typewriting, commercial arithmetic and bookkeeping is offered for the whole year. The work in typewriting consists of one practice period each day throughout the year. Definite requirements must be met in ability to manipulate a machine, in speed and in form. Class work in arithmetic and bookkeeping covers the entire year.

Credit—One unit.

EDUCATION

Child Study—The purpose of this, a second course in psychology, is to give those who are planning to teach a more thorough knowledge of the child's general nature than they deduce from the elementary course. Each student is required to make a thorough study of at least one child during the term. The children from the first four grades of the model school may be used for this purpose. The work includes a study of the significance of classroom and playground games; the order of development of the various instincts and the relative influence of heredity and environment. This course aims to familiarize the student with the mental changes of the normal child due to progress in intelligence and to advance in age.

Text—Kirkpatrick's Individual in the Making. Credit—One-third unit, or two and one-half hours. Mr. Kenamond.

Educational Measurements—The purpose of this course is to lift teaching out of the realm of opinion into the realm of science. It consists of a review of the work of such men as Thorndike, Judd and Starch to establish methods by which the product of classroom teaching may be seientifically and accurately measured by means of tests and scales. Practice in the use of most of the available tests is given. Other topics are the fineness of the marking scale and proper distribution of grades.

Text—Starch's Educational Measurements or Chapman and Rush's Scientific Measurement of Classroom Products. Credit—One-third unit, or three hours. Mr. Kenamond.

Elementary Psychology—Psychology is the most fundamental of all the professional studies and is therefore open to the senior "short course" and junior normal classes. This is the foundation course for all the more technical subjects in the department of education. Since the mind has a physiological basis, a thorough knowledge is prerequisite to this course. A physical director can scarcely hope to succeed in developing strong bodies without some knowledge of the ways by which the body grows and develops, neither can one hope to succeed in developing a mind if he does not understand at least something of the laws of mental growth. It is the purpose of this course to acquaint the pupil with the more simple mental processes. Some of the more important topics considered are the nervous system, instinct, sensation, attention, association, perception, memory, imagination, reasoning, habit, feeling, emotcn, action and will. Individual introspection is used continuously to verify the facts presented by the text. The pupil is led to improve his own mental habits and processes while studying them.

Text—The Mind and Its Education, by Betts. Credit—One-third unit, or three hours. Mr. Bond.

Ethics—The different theories of the moral standard are considered. A more extended study of our moral obligations is made, together with an investigation into that part of human life that goes out into action—that is, conduct. The moral principle is ever kept in view. In this way man's relation to his fellow-man and to God is brought out, and the duty of right living is emphasized.

Text—Brownlee's Character Building in the School, and a book on

Practical Etiquette.   Credit—One-third unit, or two and one-half hours.
Mrs. Gardiner.

History of Education—This study provides for the general survey of
the rise and progress of education and the educational systems of ancient,
mediaeval and modern states; the consideration of these in relation to one
another; how each developed alone or from some other and the influence
wielded by each system in the development of the country to which it
belongs.

With this object in view, a study is made of the educational ideas and
of the means provided for education by the Greeks and Romans; the educational ideas of the Middle Ages, the rise of the Monastic, Scholastic
and University systems, the Renaissance, Humanism and the Jesuitical
schools; educational reformers and their work, including the study of the
work of Rabelais, Montaigne, Ratich, Comenius, Rosseau, Froebel and
Pestalozzi; and finally a comparative and critical study of the educational
systems of the leading countries of the modern day, with a view to the
better understanding of the excellencies and defects in our own.

Text—A Student's History of Education, by Graves.   Credit—One-
third unit, or three hours.   Mr. Kenamond.

How to Study—There are certain very definite laws of study, a knowledge of which makes possible an economic use of time.   The purpose of
this course is to give the student a knowledge of these laws and to drill
him in their use.   Prefaces, table of contents, marginal headings, topic
sentences, setting the problem, relative values, organization of materials,
synopses and using of ideas are a few of the many topics studied.   The
method of study best adapted to the various subjects is an important part
of the work.   This course ought to be the first professional subject studied,
since it will make possible a great saving of energy expenditure.

Text—McMurry's How to Study and Teaching How to Study.   Credit
—One-third unit, or three hours.   Mr. Bond.

Hygiene and Sanitation—This course deals with personal hygiene and
sanitary conditions in the home and school.   The text book is used only
as a basis for study; numerous library references are assigned as well as
government and health society pamphlets.

Text—Ritchie's Primer of Sanitation.   Credit—One-third unit, or two
and one-half hours.   Mr. Miller.

Methods—The purpose of these courses in special methods is to review briefly the subject matter of the various subjects taught in the public
schools and to acquaint the student with the best methods of presenting
this material.

I.   The first course deals chiefly with the methods of teaching reading
and composition.   A conscious effort is made to improve the reading of
the members of the class.   Observation of type lessons is a part of the
work of this term.

Text—Briggs and Coffman's Reading in the Public Schools.

II. Arithmetic and geography are taken up during this term. The work in arithmetic consists of a review of all the important principles given in the ordinary grammar school arithmetic, with full explanation of the best methods of presentation. Special care is taken to make the student understand the psychology that lies at the basis of all the number combinations. Many special devices for securing speed and accuracy in the lower grades are discussed. The "Courtis Tests" are explained and used. Methods for securing drill and uses of diagrams are also carefully considered.

Text—Stamper's or Brown and Coffman's Methods in Arithmetic.

The last month of the term is given to a brief review of the more important points of geography, together with methods for teaching them. The large possibility of correlating geography with other subjects is emphasized. Other topics considered are pictures, maps, charts, product maps and tables, geography museums, product stories, imaginary trips and supplementary geographical reading.

Text—Principles and Methods of Teaching Geography, by Holtz.

III. The third term's work in special methods is given to the study of history and civics and to agriculture and nature study. The more important aids to history teaching which are considered are dramatization, biography, stories, art of questioning, grouping useful dates, note books and local history. Each student is expected to prepare a talk on some important historical topic. The purpose of this is to familiarize him with sources and to give him some practice n assembling material.

Text—Wayland's How to Teach American History.

The work in agriculture and nature study is for the purpose of helping the student to organize the material studied in the more extensive courses in agriculture and biology around problems suited to children in rural and graded schools. Field excursions are taken. All students taking this course are required to belong to the bird club or some other organization, the purpose of which is the systematic study of nature.

Credit—One unit, or eight hours, for the year's work. Mr. Bond.

Observation and Teaching—The Board of Education of Shepherdstown District, Jefferson County, has granted to Shepherd College the privilege of using the Shepherdstown Graded School of eight separate grades and the several schools of the district for observation and practice work. By this arrangement all members of the senior class are enabled to get some practice in applying the theories learned in the other professional courses and in meeting the real problems of the schoolroom under the guidance of experienced and sympathetic teachers who are in charge of these various schools.

During the fall term the observation work is carried on in connection with the course in Special Methods. The classes go in a body to observe special type lessons taught by the regular teachers. Members of the class are urged to visit at other periods as opportunity offers. Each student taking this work must teach one lesson, the plan of which has been approved both by the teacher in charge of the room where the lesson is to be taught and by the teacher in the Normal who has charge of the Methods classes.

During the winter term more systematic work in observation and teaching is undertaken. Some students are required to teach one room for two or three consecutive days; others are required to teach one subject, perhaps, for one week. This teaching work is arranged so as to interfere as little as possible with the student's other work. The amount and kind of teaching is not meant to be uniform, but rather to meet the needs of each student as determined by his individual successes. Twice each week all members of the class meet for a systematic discussion of observation and of practice work.

During the spring term there is a continuation of the observation and practice work during the winter. Special attention is given to the treatment of abnormal or exceptional children. Special programs and the best methods of preparing them are studied carefully.

Credit—One-half unit, or four hours. Mr. Bond.

Pedagogy—"The individual teacher must have a part in the construction of the science in which his art is to have its foundations." How large a part this is to be must necessarily depend upon his analytical knowledge of human nature and his capacity for logical and synthetic thinking. Most aspirants for the teaching profession do not possess knowledge requisite for taking a very large part in this constructive work, but must seek guidance and reinforcement in scientific treatises on the subject. To supply these essentials is the aim of the course. After a thorough review of psychological principles the problem of the correlation of studies and best methods of teaching them is taken up, as are also the principles of instruction, knowledge and culture underlying each of them.

Text—Strayer's The Teaching Process. Credit—One-third unit, or two and one-half hours. Mr. Bond.

Rural Education—This course is offered for the special benefit of those who are planning to teach in the rural schools. Some of the many topics for study are as follows: Attendance, adapting the state course to local needs, adapting the subject matter of the texts to the interests of the children, grading and classification, devices for saving time, home-made helps and apparatus, relation of the teacher to the supervisor, responsibility of the teacher to the community socially, methods for helping the adult members of society, possibilities and advantages of consolidation, and correlation of the school with the other educative institutions of the community.

Text—Better Rural Schools, by Betts and Hall, or Wilkinson's Rural School Management. Credit—One-third unit, or two and one-half hours. **Mr. Kenamond.**

TEACHER'S REVIEW CLASS

Rural Sociology—The purpose of this course is to give to the student a proper estimate of conditions as they exist in the rural sections of the State, to enable him to make a correct survey of his local affairs, to arouse him to a higher appreciation of the joys and privileges of country life, and to suggest ways and means of making the country life all that it may be by a proper application of the principles of right living.

Text—Fiske's Challenge of the Country. Credit—One-third unit, or two and one-half hours. Mr. Muldoon.

School Administration—As the basis of this course the excellent book, "Our Schools: Their Administration and Supervision," by William E. Chancellor, is used. Here are defined and discussed the sphere and duties of boards of education, superintendents, principals, supervisors and class teachers. The state system of education, the private school, course of study, salary, tenure and certification—all come in for their share of attention.

Credit—One-third unit, or two and one-half hours. Mr. Miller.

School Management—This subject places emphasis upon the personality of the teacher, his preparation and responsibility, the daily schedule, school government, treatment of school evils, proper use of examinations and other subjects of vital interest to those preparing to teach.

Text—Seeley's New School Management. Credit—One-third unit, or two and one-half hours. Mr. Miller.

Social Education—Education is fundamentally a social process. This course deals with some of the more important social aspects of the school. The first half of the course is given largely to a study of such questions as the following: The individual's relation to society; the educational significance of institutions; the social significance of play in school life; the importance of avocations; the social origin and organization of the curriculum.

The second half of the course is given to a study of concrete examples illustrating the various aspects of social education. The method of study and the method of conducting the class both seek to emphasize in concrete form the principles studied. Each student is required to make a brief social investigation of some topic of local interest.

Text—Social Principles of Education, by Betts. Credit—One-third unit, or two and one-half hours. Mr. Bond.

Sociology—This is a study of modern social problems as they relate to present day educational problems.

Text—Ellwood's Modern Social Problems. Credit—One-third unit, or two and one-half hours. Mr. Miller.

For additional courses in education, see Art III., English XIV. and XV. Public School Music and Nature Study.

ENGLISH

English—I, II, III. The English work in this year comprises gram-mar, composition and literature. Three periods each week are devoted to a study of grammar; one to composition and one to literature. In the grammar work special emphasis is laid upon the study of the sentence and upon training the student to use correct English. Careful study is made of verbs, infinitives and participles and of the principles of sentence con-struction.

One theme each week throughout the year, and at least one book re-port each term are required. In all composition work careful attention is paid to proper development of the paragraph. Themes are read in class and are criticized by both instructor and pupils. A number of themes are based on the literature work.

The following classics are read and studied: The Great Stone Face, The Man Without a Country, Evangeline, Hiawatha, Courtship of Miles Standish, and other narrative poems.

Texts—Prince's Grammar and Buhlig's Business English. Credit— One unit. Miss Smith.

English—IV, V, VI. Rhetoric is the basis for the work of this year. The work in rhetoric includes a study of the sentence, the paragraph and the theme. Special attention is paid to unity, coherence and emphasis. A study is made of the forms of discourse. Examples of each form are presented to the class, and the characteristic features of each are pointed out and discussed. Some attention is given to a study of versification and to figures of speech.

Two themes and at least one oral composition are required each week. Much attention is paid to criticism of written work. The themes are read in class, and the members of the class as well as the teacher offer criti-cisms. At least two long papers and one book report are required each term.

The following classics are studied and a part of the composition work is based upon them: Silas Marner, As You Like It, Shorter English Poems, including Gray's Elegy, The Deserted Village, The Prisoner of Chillon, Sohrab and Rustum, and Lays of Ancient Rome. Stevenson's Inland Voyage and Travels with a Donkey are read in class.

Texts—Scott and Denny's New Composition and Rhetoric; Woolley's Handbook of Composition. Credit—One unit. Miss Turner.

English—VII, VIII, IX. The basis for this year's work is American Literature. The chief aim is to develop in the student an appreciation of what is truly great in our literature and to stimulate his love for reading so that he will be constantly adding to his knowledge of literature after he leaves school.

Three periods each week are spent on the study of Long's American Poems and selected poems of Longfellow, Emerson, Bryant, Whittier,

Lowell and Poe; Washington's Farewell Address, Webster's Bunker Hill Oration, Emerson's Essays and Poe's Tales. Franklin's Autobiography and Irving's Tales of a Traveler are read in class. Blount's Intensive Studies is used in connection with the study of classics.

One period is spent each week in the study of Halleck's American Literature.

One theme a week is required and one recitation period is devoted to a study of the principles of composition, special attention being paid to description and narration. At least two long papers are written by the student each term. Written and oral reports of assigned readings are frequently made.

Credit—One unit. Miss Turner.

English—X, XI, XII. The text for the work of this year is Halleck's English Literature. The same period of time is spent on the text-book and on composition as in the preceding year's work. Special attention is paid to exposition and argumentation.

Three periods a week are spent in the study of the following classics: Chaucer's Prologue, Shakespeare's Merchant of Venice and Twelfth Night, Milton's Minor Poems and Paradise Lost (Books I and II), Carlyle's Essay on Burns, Coleridge's Ancient Mariner, Tennyson's Princess and Idylls of the King (four), Selections from Wordsworth and Browning. Child's Translation of Beowulf and Spenser's Faerie Queene are read in class.

Credit—One unit. Miss Turner.

English—XIII. Advanced Rhetoric. A close study is made of the forms of discourse by means of analysis of specimens and practice in writing. Three themes a week and four long papers are required of each student. This course is based on Holt's Specimens of the Forms of Discourse and Canby and Opdycke's Elements of Composition.

Credit—One-third unit, or three hours. Miss Turner.

English—XIV. Methods of Teaching Language. Careful attention is given to methods of teaching grammar and composition in the grades. The members of the class are required to make out lesson plans and to present model lessons.

Text—Klapper's The Teaching of English. Credit—One-third unit, or two and one-half hours. Miss Turner.

English XV. Literature in the Grades. The aim of this course is to acquaint students with literature that is suitable for children in the grades. A study is made of typical specimens of literature. Practice teaching is an important part of the course. The children in the various grades are made acquainted with literature through story telling and the dramatizing of simple classics.

Text—Lowe's Literature for Children. Credit—One-third unit, or two and one-half hours. Miss Turner.

Orthography—Orthography is taught during the entire course, special effort being made to have every student in the school become an accurate and proficient speller and an intelligent user of the dictionary. To this end spelling recitations, both written and oral, are given three days out of the week throughout the year. In connection with the spelling the origin, derivation, properties and meanings of the words spelled are given attention, and diacritical marking is mastered.

Reed's Word Lessons and the Modern Spelling Book are the texts used in the first two years. No credit.

Rhetoricals—On each Monday, and occupying an hour and a quarter of time, each teacher has a literary exercise in his room, consisting of reading, essays, orations, debates, current history, etc. To this end students are classified at the beginning of each year and assigned to the various teachers, the assignment depending on the advancement of the student. No credit.

EXPRESSION

Mrs. Gibson

Since natural expression must proceed from a sound mind in a sound body, the first year's work consists of physical culture, relaxation and contraction exercises for repose and harmony of action; voice culture for strength, purity and distinctness, training the imagination to see the thought and hold it in mind while portraying it for others; cultivation of the memory to retain the thought and acquire the language of the author; sight reading and recitation; and the preparation and recital of a required number of selections.

This course does not consist merely of a lot of exercises and rules of elocution, but principles and laws of expression applied to conversation and recitation; the pupil is led to recognize these whenever he meets them in speech and on the printed page. This makes it an interesting study and is of great assistance in other studies. An excellent opportunity of appearing before an audience is afforded in the weekly meetings of the literary societies, while public recitals are held by the department whenever practicable.

Credit—One-third unit, or two and one-half hours. Tuition for individual instruction, $10 per term.

FRENCH

Mr. Duke

French I.—Elementary French. Introduction of Chardenal's Complete French Course. Exercises in reading, spelling, pronunciation.

II.—Elementary French. A continuation of Course I. Continuation of Chardenal's French Grammar. Translation of exercises from English into French and vice versa, reading in class and introduction to composition work. Oral exercises to make the student familiar with the sounds of the language and to establish the correct pronunciation. Reading of Joyne's "French Fairy Tales."

III.—Elementary French. A continuation of Course II. Chardenal's Grammar finished. Extensive exercises in translating English into French. French conversation and the thorough study of the irregular verbs and their use in speech and life. Reading of Rollin's French Reader.

Credit—One unit, or eight hours, for the year. Offered 1917-1918, and alternate years.

French IV.—Introduction of the works of celebrated modern French authors and writers, such as Daudet, Dumas, Audre, Theuriet, etc. Grandgent's composition based on "Le Siege de Berlin." During these reading exercises the student is kept in touch with the grammar, and the most common expressions in the French language are drilled upon.

V.—Extensive composition work. Discussion of grammatical points in connection with the translation. Translation and study of Merimee's "Colomba."

VI.—Prose reading. Rapid reading of large amount of prose to render the student familiar with the idioms of the language. Works by About, Dumas, La Martine and others.

Credit—One unit, or eight hours, for the year. Offered 1918-1919, and alternate years.

GERMAN

Mr. Duke

German I.—Grammar, reading and composition. This course, in fact, all of the three courses embracing the first year's work, is designed to give the student a good pronouncing, reading and working knowledge of the more elementary part of the language. Special attention is given its pronunciation, inflection, and the acquiring of a vocabulary.

Texts—Thomas' Practical German Grammar, Super's Elementary German Reader, Part I.

II.—A continuation of Course I. Super's Reader continued. Special attention is given to correct spelling, pronunciation and composition work.

III.—In this course special attention is given to the translation of German into English, the work being based on Hervey's Elementary Exercises to Thomas' German Grammar. Seidel's "Die Monate" and Bacon's "Im Vaterland" are also read.

Credit—One unit, or eight hours, for the year. Offered 1916-1917, and succeeding alternate years.

German IV.—German Prose: Copious reading of German prose to render the student familiar with the idioms of the language and to give a large and varied vocabulary. Heyse's "L'Arrabbiata;" Hillern's "Hoher als die Kirche;" Schiller's "Der Neffe als Onkel;" Storm's "Immensee."

V.—Composition. Practice in writing German and translating English prose into German. Discussion of grammatical points in connection with the translation. Study of the irregular verbs. Reading at sight. Harris' Prose Composition. Thomas' Practical Grammar, Part II.

VI.—Reading and memorizing of a great number of short well-known poems. Von Klenze's "Deutsche Gedichte." Translation of Goethe's "Herrmann und Dorothea." Extensive practice in conversation, to make the student familiar with the sound and expression of the language, is given.

Credit—One unit, or eight hours, for the year. Offered 1917-1918, and succeeding alternate years.

HISTORY AND ECONOMICS

Mrs. Gardiner

The purpose of this department is to teach a reasonable number of the facts of history; to help the student to classify and organize these facts; to cultivate the judgment; to show how the present has grown out of the past and how the future may best be served by it; to show the relation between literature and history; and, incidentally, to teach the student the use of books and libraries.

The method of instruction is different in the several courses. No one method is followed exclusively. A standard text is used as the basis of work, which is supplemented by much outside work on the part of the students. Definite topics are assigned and reported upon by the students.

Note books are kept in most of the courses. Map studies and picture studies are made helpful. Sources and source material are used to a limited extent. Papers and bibliographies on special subjects aid materially in carrying on the work.

Ancient History—This course is introduced by a brief study of Eastern nations, special attention being given to their origin, their growth and development, and their contributions to progress.

In connection with the history of Greece, her debt to the Eastern nations and her political history are studied. Emphasis is placed on her gifts in the fields of art, literature, philosophy, etc.

The Hellenistic period serves as a stepping stone to Roman history. Stress is laid upon Rome's contribution to the world in politics and legal science. The text used is Robinson and Breasted's Outlines of European History, Volume 1.

Credit—One-third unit.

Mediaeval History—After a review of events from the German migration to Charlemange in 800, the great events such as feudalism, the investiture strife, mediaeval church, development of the Papacy, the renaissance are taken up and studied in order. This course closes with the death of Louis XIV. Emphasis is laid upon the rise of the modern nations. Robinson and Breasted's Outlines of European History, Volume 1.

Credit—One-third unit.

Modern History—The two courses in modern history are a continuation of the mediaeval history from the death of Louis XIV. to the present time. The work centers around the Protestant Revolution, the French Revolution, the unification of Germany and Italy. The aim is to give the best understanding of the world politics of today. Robinson and Beard's European History, Volume 2.

Credit—Two-thirds unit, for the two courses.

Mythology—Mythology is taught for its own sake and as a basis for literature. An effort is made to show the meaning and beauty of the Greek and other myths and legends studied, and to stimulate interest in these concrete ideals of the ancients, both for their bearing on the literature and life of these peoples, and also for their influence on modern literature and others.

Text—Gayley's Classic Myths. Credit—One-third unit.

History of England—This course will trace the history of England from the earliest time to the present, emphasizing chiefly the beginning of the representative government, the growth and decline of Feudalism, the rise of the Commons and the transition from arbitrary to constitutional monarchy.

Text—Coman and Kendall. Credit—One-third unit.

American History—American History is studied from the earliest explorations and settlements up to the present time. The aim of this course, taking up as it does a study of the growth and development of the nation and government, is to make patriotic citizens.

Text—Bourne and Benton. Credit—One-third unit.

Civics—In this course there is first a survey of the leading facts in the history of our country. This review prepares the way for a careful study of the origin and development of our political institutions. The two subjects, history and civil government, are studied in close connection with each other. The aim is to enlist the interests of the student in social welfare, to point out the intimate relation between civics and life.

Text—Forman's American Republic. Credit—One-third unit.

West Virginia History—The object is to acquaint our young people with the story of our great commonwealth.

Credit—One-third unit.

Bible History—The purpose is to give a historical study of the Bible, which is somewhat of a review of parts of Ancient History.

Text—Blaikie's History of the Bible. Credit—One-third unit, or two and one-half hours.

Library Science—This course is to acquaint the student with the aids found in the library and classification and arrangement of books.

Credit—One-third unit, or two and one-half hours.

Economics—In economics one course is presented. It has for its purpose the training of the student to think correctly and independently along economic lines. He is led to see the actual economic facts that are about him, taught how to treat with them, how to classify them and discover their relations. Some attention is paid to the fundamental principles underlying the production, exchange, distribution and consumption of wealth. The principles of taxation and hence the sources of revenue, and the expenditure of public funds, are closely studied. Socialism, trades and labor unions, monopolies, public and private, co-operative and benevolent associations, etc., all receive attention.

Text—Burch and Nearing. Credit—One-third unit, or three hours.

HOME ECONOMICS

Miss Cowsill

Pending events demand that very definite measures be taken if the women of the country are to be prepared to meet the emergencies that confront. Special stress is laid upon this in the classes in domestic science.

Home comfort depends upon the ability of the housewife to convert with ease the raw materials for use and decoration. The power to do this is acquired through training. The construction of articles made in the domestic art class will secure a better product and a better standard than can be obtained in the "ready-mades" and at the same time develop in the girl the power to do.

In the sewing course no time is lost on samples, but from the very first lesson instruction is given on full-sized articles. Various stitches are taught as the work progresses. Special emphasis is laid on correct finishing and economical cutting. The cost of each article is calculated before making and economy and service are given special consideration.

Home Economics I.—Conservation of food—Home preservation of food. This course includes a series of lessons treating of the storage, drying and canning of all surplus food products, also the working out of recipes in which dried food products are used.

Sewing projects—Hand towel, laundry bag, pillow cases, pad for mattress, sheets, comforter (class piece), dresser cover, curtains.

Textiles—This subject includes a study of all materials in sewing. Various kinds of weaves are studied by the students so that they may be able to discriminate between the different fabrics. Experiments are made to show the common adulterations for textile fabrics.

Four double periods for laboratory. One single period for theory.

Texts—Shelter and Clothing, by Kinne and Cooley, and Foods and Household Management. Credit—One-third unit, or three hours.

Home Economics II.—Problems of substitutes, utilization of left-overs, preparation of school lunch.

SNAP SHOTS OF SCHOOL FAIR AND PARADE

Sewing—Work set—cap and apron—set of underclothes, shirt waist.

The home—Aims of a home, ideals in establishing a home.

Texts—Shelter and Clothing, by Kinne and Cooley, and Foods and Household Management. Credit—One-third unit, or two and one-half hours.

Home Economics III.—Menus and dietaries, planning and serving of meals, infant feeding, invalid cookery.

Sewing—School dress, graduation dress.

Practice teaching once a week. Lessons in simple cooking and sewing in the seventh and eighth grades.

Texts—Food and Household Management, and Shelter and Clothing, by Kinne and Cooley. Credit—One-third unit, or two and one-half hours.

LATIN

Miss Smith

The course in Latin is arranged to enable the student who expects to attend college to meet the entrance requirements for standard colleges and universities. The work as outlined covers three years. Cicero's Oration for Archias and Oration for the Manilian Law, which are not provided for in the regular course, are read in a special class under the direct supervision of the instructor.

Two years of language work are required for graduation in the Secondary and regular Normal Course. The object of this study of Latin is to give the student greater insight into language structure and thus enable him to be more proficient as a teacher of English Grammar in the elementary school course. Careful attention is given to pronunciation, English derivation and grammatical construction, constant comparisons being made with English grammar. In addition to this the language is studied from the viewpoint of literature and Roman life and customs.

The courses are outlined as follows:

Latin I.—Smith's Latin Lessons.

II.—A continuation of Course I.

III.—Completion of text, with Caesar, Book I, Chapters 1-14.

Credit—One unit, for the year.

Latin IV.—Caesar's Gallic War (Books I, II).

V.—Caesar's Gallic War (Books III, IV), Cicero's First Oration against Catiline.

VI.—Cicero's Second, Third and Fourth Orations against Catiline.

Barss' Latin Prose Composition is used throughout the second year.

Credit—One unit, for the year.

Latin VII.—Virgil's Æneid (Books I, II).

VIII.—Virgil's Æneid (Books III, IV).

IX.—Virgil's Æneid (Books V, VI).

Metrical reading and mythology throughout the year.

Bennett's Latin Grammar is used for reference. Comstock's edition of Virgil is recommended and any standard text in Caesar and Cicero will be accepted.

Credit—One unit, or eight hours, for the year. Offered 1917-1918, and succeeding alternate years.

MANUAL TRAINING

Mr. McBrien

Class work will consist of two forty-five minute periods a day, five days in the week, and to obtain credit for any work done in this department at least two terms' work must be taken.

Mechanical drawing will be correlated with the shop work and will include the use and care of instruments, geometric drawings, projections, working drawings, blue printing and working drawings of the projects to be made in the shop.

In the shop exercises will be given in making the joints, important to the carpenter and the cabinet maker, and later applied in the construction of articles for practical use. Instruction will be given in the squaring, gauging, sawing, boring, planing, chiseling, fitting, gluing, sandpapering and finishing in the construction of articles useful in the school or home. During the latter part of the work students are given the opportunity to construct pieces of furniture, etc., from drawings made by them in the drawing class.

Stress will also be laid on whittling, coping saw work and projects suitable for the use of teachers in the graded schools where little equipment is required or can be procured.

Throughout the year periods will be devoted to the study of such topics as bench tools, woodworking machinery, timber, including growth, milling, uses, strength, method of finishing, etc., the carpenter's square, etc.

Text—Griffith's Principles of Woodworking. Credit—One unit, or eight hours, for the year.

MATHEMATICS

Arithmetic—Credit towards graduation is given for one term's work in Arithmetic. The aim of the work done is to train the pupil to have an understanding of the few simple principles involved in all work in arithmetic and to have him avoid blindly following certain rules without understanding the principles underlying them. An effort is made to have the work as practical as possible, that the pupils may be able to solve the problems that deal with common, everyday life.

Credit—One-third unit.

Algebra I.—Literal notation, the equation, factors, monomials, polynomials, relative numbers, addition, subtraction, multiplication, and type products.

II.—Division, equations of one unknown, fractions, ratio, proportion, variation, factoring.

III.—Equations, graphical work, systems of equations of two, three or more unknowns, quadratic equations, radicals and exponents, involution and evolution.

Text—Young and Jackson's First Course. Credit—One unit, for the year. Mr. Duke.

Algebra IV.—Review of first year work, advanced work on subjects covered in second and third terms. Logarithms, imaginary and complex numbers, variation, series. An elective course.

Text—Young and Jackson's Second Course. Credit—One-third unit. Mr. Kenamond. Offered 1916-1917, and succeeding alternate years.

Plane Geometry—The most careful accuracy is required in geometry as well as in all other mechanical work. The student is required to thoroughly understand each step before proceeding to the next higher. The study of Geometry is successful only when the student has been thoroughly imbued with the importance of accurate methods. Once he is led to realize the value of doing things just right and no other way, he has received a training which must sooner or later bring him success.

The fundamental theorems of the line, the angle, the triangle, the quadrilateral, polygon, regular and irregular, and circle, in plane geometry, are thoroughly understood. The exercises in the texts are required to be solved as completely as the theorems.

I. Rectilinear figures, and circle to measurement of angles.

II. Measurement of angles of circles, construction of circles, theory of proportion, similar polygons.

III. Areas of polygons, regular polygons, measurement of the circle.

Text—Wells and Hart's Plane Geometry. Credit—One unit, for the year. Mr. Kenamond.

Solid Geometry—The same method is pursued in this course as in plane geometry. Practical examples and original exercises throughout the course. This is an elective course.

Text—New Solid Geometry, by Wells. Credit—One-third unit, or three hours. Mr. Kenamond. Offered 1916-1917, and succeeding alternate years.

Trigonometry—The practical value of Trigonometry is very great, since it is essential to the work of surveying, astronomy and, indeed, to all sciences which depend upon mathematical demonstrations. Trigonometry treats of the relations of lines and angles by algebraic methods. An elective course.

Text—Wells. Credit—One-third unit, or two and one-half hours. Mr. Kenamond. Offered in 1916-1917, and succeeding alternate years.

MUSIC

Miss Merrells

The Department of Music offers instruction in piano, voice, pipe organ, harmony and history of music.

Candidates for a teacher's certificate in piano must have completed Fillmore's Musical History and three courses in Harmony in addition to the following thorough foundation in technique, studies, etc.

Piano I.—Studies by Heller, Czerny, Cramer and Mendelssohn; Bach's Two-part Inventions, concertos and sonatas by Mozart, Schubert and Haydn.

Piano II.—Bach's Three-part Inventions, Hanon and Cramer studies; pieces by Brahms, Chopin, Mozkowski andd MacDowell, adapted to the needs of the pupil.

Piano III.—Beethoven Sonatas, concertos by Mendelssohn, Book II. Haydn and pieces by Brahms, Raff, Rubenstein and Tschaikowsky.

Piano IV.—Chopin's Polonaises, Grieg's Holberg Suite, Bach's Preludes and Fugues and selections from Wagner, Schumann and Liszt. One concerto to be memorized.

This course is used as a basis, but ambitious students may finish the course in less than four years, depending upon the time spent at work and upon the talent of the individual.

Public recitals and concerts are given frequently, which develop confidence in playing in public. Studio recitals are given by the pupils who are not so far advanced.

Vocal Music—The Girls' Glee Club and the Mixed Chorus offer excellent opportunities in vocal drill. These organizations assist in the concerts.

A course in public school music, twice a week during the fall and winter term, is open to seniors in the normal course. Credit—Two hours.

Tuition in piano courses, 50 cents a lesson. There are four practice pianos for the free use of music students. Knabe and Haines Brothers pianos are used exclusively in this institution.

SCIENCE

Geography—Each year the need for more emphasis upon the study of Geography becomes noticeable. The economic study of this subject must influence the student to a higher appreciation of his fellow man and make him realize more fully the part he is to take in the affairs of life.

I. Physical Geography. Following a fair preparation of what is commonly called Political Geography, this subject naturally falls. In some measure this division of the subject is informational, but the aim is to make the student more appreciative of the part geographical conditions have to do with the growth, development, characteristics, habits, manner and life of the human family. By observation, references and study of concrete cases as they come the work is done.

Text—Gilbert and Brigham's Physical Geography.

II. Commercial Geography. This course is conducted on the inductive plan. Taking several industries as examples, the principles of Commercial Geography are evolved and the student comes into a knowledge of the various forms of geographical influences which have so much to do with fixing the life, character and habits of a people.

Text—Brigham's Commercial Geography.

III. Industrial Geography. In much the same way as in the above course the student is made to know the conditions which affect the industrial life of the United States and the country at large. Life in all its bearings to industry and to the economic worth of a country is emphasized. By reference, observation and concrete examples the work is done.

Credit—One unit, for the year. Mr. Muldoon.

Biology—Through the study of plants, the lower forms of animal life, and then human life, the student comes into a proper appreciation of the relations of all living things to each other. The equipment for this work has been enhanced by the special laboratory and new apparatus.

The laboratory work is emphasized and things are studied and at all times the text is merely directional.

I. Plant Biology. The study of life begins with plants. The school garden furnishes abundant material for this work. By demonstration and by experiment the composition, function, economic value and reproduction of plants are shown. A higher appreciation of the beautiful in nature is emphasized.

II. Animal Biology. The study of the lower animals is taken up in this course. Types of various forms of animal life are studied. The functions of the organs, the economic value of the animal, reproduction, etc., are studied by observation, demonstration, and the text.

III. Human Biology. With the preparation of the two courses preceding, the student is prepared to take up the study of the highest form of animal life, and it is done with all seriousness and without hesitation. The course is designed to give the student a proper appreciation of the various organs of the human system, their function and care, and to emphasize his responsibility.

Text—Smallwood. Credit—One unit, for the year. Mr. Muldoon.

Physics—Throughout the year the work consists of four recitations or demonstration lessons and at least two hours of laboratory work per week. The individual experimental work is constantly under the supervision and direction of the instructor. Thirty-two representative experiments are on the required list. A note-book record of the work is taken at the time of the experiment and later written up and submitted for permanent record. Laboratory handbook, Millikan, Gale and Bishop.

I. Properties of matter, mechanics of solids, gases, heat and work.

II. Magnetism, static electricity, current electricity to induced **currents.**

III. Induced currents, sound and light.

Text—Millikan and Gale's First Course, Revised. Credit—One unit, for the year. Mr. Kenamond.

Chemistry—There are three recitations and class demonstrations per week and three hours of laboratory work. The experimental work takes up McPherson and Henderson's Laboratory Exercises in Chemistry, following the order of the text, and is intended for the most part to precede and form the basis of class recitations.

The work in chemistry deals largely with the inorganic compounds. About three weeks are spent on common organic compounds.

Quantitative work on water and air. Qualitative tests for various elements. Mathematical exercises in gravimetric and volumetric relations, correction for temperature and pressure, and balancing of equations. Bearing of chemistry on agriculture, home economics and every-day life is carefully noted.

I. Chemical theory. Oxygen, hydrogen, nitrogen.

II. Non-metals. Organic compounds and foods.

III. Metals and fertilizers. .

Text—McPherson and Henderson's First Course in Chemistry. Credit —One unit, for the year. Mr. Kenamond.

Agriculture—The intention of the work is to give students an opportunity to get possession of some of the primary truths of the science and at the same time acquire some idea as to how the subject should be presented to a class of students in the elementary schools of the State. The DeLaval Separator Company have placed at our disposal one of their machines. A school garden has been added to the equipment and demonstrative school gardening is made a part of the course in the Spring Term.

I. General Agriculture. This course is primary and extensive in its nature. It is aimed to get a general view of the entire subject in all its various phases. This course is given in the Fall Term and Spring Term.

Text—Waters' Principles of Agriculture.

II. Animal Husbandry. This course is designed to make a closer study of farm animal life. Among the topics studied are types of horses, cattle, swine; feeds and feeding; care and breeding of farm stock; dairying, etc.

Text—Harper's Animal Husbandry for Schools.

III. Farm Crops. This course takes up the various farm crops fitted to West Virginia soil and climate and deals with the preparation of the seed bed, selection of the seed, cultivation, harvesting, disposition of the crop, etc. Orcharding is emphasized.

Text—Agee's Crops and Methods for Soil Improvement.

Credit—One unit, or eight hours, for the year. Mr. Muldoon.

Nature Study.—This course in Nature Study is divided into three distinct parts: (*a*) A study of the underlying principles and methods which results in a just appreciation of the purpose of Nature Study and ways of presenting the subject to pupils in the grades. Model lessons are taught to pupils of the various grades by students and their work criticised. (*b*) The second part of the course is intended to furnish teachers with subject matter of a biological nature with hints and suggestions on the collection and care of material for lessons. (*c*) The last part of the course consists of a course of Nature Study for the grades in which materials and methods of presentation are furnished for each grade in the average school.

Text—Holtz. Credit—One-third unit, or three hours. Mr. Muldoon.

Enrollment of Students, 1916-1917

Under the title "Terms," F means fall term, W means winter term and S means spring term. Students for the summer term are listed separately.

SENIORS — NORMAL

Name	Post Office — County	Terms
Bell, Agnes Mae	Shepherdstown, Jefferson	FWS
Bussard, Agnes Marguerite	Harpers Ferry, Jefferson	FWS
Canfield, Virginia Pascal	Paw Paw, Morgan	FWS
Casler, Frances Leola	Berkeley Springs, Morgan	WS
Foltz, Cozy Gladys	Martinsburg, Berkeley	FWS
Kiser, Della Grace	Alaska, Mineral	F
Lindsay, Margaret Isabella	Sandy Spring, Md., Montg'y	FWS
Payne, Grace Fleming	Hedgesville, Berkeley	FWS
Rockenbaugh, Cora Adelle	Harpers Ferry, Jefferson	FWS
Scott, Ethel Fay	Parsons, Tucker	FWS
VanZandt, Agnes Mae	Newburg, Preston	FWS
Bell, Ellis, Clifton	Bardane, Jefferson	FWS
Lowry, Hubert David	Springdale, Fayette	FWS
Ours, Lester	Petersburg, Grant	FWS
Shanholtzer, James Clinton	Hanging Rock, Hampshire	FWS
Williamson, Max Miller	Shepherdstown, Jefferson	FWS
Wolford, Feaster	Dry Fork, Tucker	FWS

SENIORS — SHORT COURSE

Name	Post Office — County	Terms
Athey, Olive Butler	Shepherdstown, Jefferson	FWS
Louthan, Frances Rachel	Shepherdstown, Jefferson	FWS
Needy, Mary Catherine	Shepherdstown, Jefferson	FWS
Offutt, Edna Venora	Augusta, Hampshire	FWS
Stanley, Lillie Virginia	Shenandoah Junct'n, Jefferson	FWS
Walker, Lola Virginia	Shepherdstown, Jefferson	FWS
Williams, Kathryn Folk	Shepherdstown, Jefferson	FWS
Williams, Nannie Louraine	Shepherdstown, Jefferson	FWS
Wynkoop, Julia Yates	Charles Town, Jefferson	FWS
Hutton, Charles Lee	Shepherdstown, Jefferson	FWS
Lemen, Wiloughby Morgan	Shepherdstown, Jefferson	FWS
Long, Andrew Fleming	Amboy, Preston	FWS
Wheaton, Earle	Shepherdstown, Jefferson	FWS

A GLIMPSE UNDER THE TREES

SENIORS — SECONDARY

Name	Post Office — County	Terms
Appel, Margaret Prudence	Paw Paw, Morgan	FWS
Kiser, William Raymond	Alaska, Mineral	FWS

JUNIORS — NORMAL

Best, Martha	Davis, Tucker	FWS
Carper, Glenna James	Churchville, Va., Augusta	FWS
Flaherty, Blanche Lacy	Madison Mills, Va., Madison	FWS
Hollida, Maude VanMetre	Martinsburg, Berkeley	FWS
Patriquin, Olive LaDelto	Horton, Randolph	FWS
Stanley, Ether May	Shenandoah Junct'n, Jefferson	F
Clark, Elmer P	Berkeley Springs, Morgan	S
Hartzell, George	Shepherdstown, Jefferson	FWS
Hendricks, Gilbert Leo	Shenandoah Junct'n, Jefferson	FWS
Myers, William Clayton, Jr	Shepherdstown, Jefferson	FWS

JUNIORS — SECONDARY

Armentrout, Ethel Vesta	Waynesboro, Va., Augusta	S
Bell, Bessie Bonnylin	Bardane, Jefferson	FWS
Carvey, Mary Susan	Alaska, Mineral	WS
Cooper, Olive	Harman, Randolph	FWS
Denison, Gertrude	Shepherdstown, Jefferson	FWS
Ewers, Lucile Johnson	Three Churches, Hampshire	FWS
Ferrell, Julia Cameron	Shepherdstown, Jefferson	FWS
Hockman, Ella Mabel	Slanesville, Hampshire	FWS
Johnson, Bessie Bay	Levels, Hampshire	FWS
Kiser, Florence Irene	Alaska, Mineral	FWS
Koontz, Helena Temple	Shepherdstown, Jefferson	FWS
Lawson, Elsie Louise	Manassas, Va., Prince Wm	S
Lemen, Lillie Virginia	Martinsburg, Berkeley	FWS
Martin, Hazel Irene	Shepherdstown, Jefferson	FWS
Muldoon, Gertrude Virginia	Shepherdstown, Jefferson	FWS
Needy, Alice Mary	Shepherdstown, Jefferson	FWS
Portmess, Fay Marie	Cacapehon, Hampshire	F
Roby, Virginia	Petersburg, Grant	FWS
Seibert, Edna Harding	Kearneysville, Berkeley	FWS
Selvey, Helen Rebecca	Shepherdstown, Jefferson	FWS
Strieby, Carrie Lucile	Shepherdstown, Jefferson	FWS
Butts, Thomas Reed	Hedgesville, Berkeley	FWS
Dearing, Alfred Willis	Shenandoah Junct'n, Jefferson	FWS
Durst, Vernon R	Levels, Hampshire	FWS

Name	Post Office — County	Terms
Engle, Kenneth Hendricks	Shenandoah Junct'n, Jefferson	FWS
Folk, J. David	Shepherdstown, Jefferson	FWS
Fulton, Sanford DeWitt	Cherry Run, Morgan	FWS
Fulton, Stanley Merritt	Cherry Run, Morgan	FWS
Hawkins, J. Allen	Wardensville, Hardy	S
Heckert, George Theodore	Breedlove, Preston	FWS
Herr, Walter Edward	Shepherdstown, Jefferson	FWS
Kretzer, Charles Cecil	Shepherdstown (Md.), Wash.	FWS
Ludwig, George P.	Rio, Hardy	S
Myers, James Howard	Martinsburg, Berkeley	FWS
Myers, John Clive	Shenandoah Junct'n, Jefferson	FWS
Myers, Reed Folk	Shepherdstown, Jefferson	FWS
Propst, Fred Michael	Brandywine, Pendleton	WS
Pyles, Norman Lamont	Shepherdstown, Jefferson	FWS
Roby, Hobart	Petersburg, Grant	FWS
Seibert, Robert Carrolton	Kearneysville, Berkeley	FWS
Snyder, Harry Lambright, Jr.	Shepherdstown, Jefferson	FWS
Thompson, James Robert	Three Churches, Hampshire	FWS
Whiting, William Bernard	Shepherdstown, Jefferson	FWS
Worman, Charles Edwin	Shepherdstown, Jefferson	FWS

SOPHOMORES

Name	Post Office — County	Terms
Bender, Edna Jane	Martinsburg, Berkeley	WS
Billmyer, Irene Hammack	Shepherdstown, Jefferson	S
Bradfield, Anna Belle	Baker, Hardy	S
Burgess, Sara Jane	Laurel Dale, Mineral	S
DeHaven, Pearl	Glengary, Berkeley	WS
Hamrick, Ethel Standiford	Shepherdstown, Jefferson	FWS
Harper, Erma	Harperton, Randolph	S
Houser, Della Virginia	Sharpsburg, Md., Washington	FW
Huyett, Sara Hortense	Charles Town, Jefferson	FWS
Johnson, Hattie Bartlett	Three Churches, Hampshire	F
Knott, Phoebe Virginia	Shepherdstown, Jefferson	FWS
Lemen, Mary Newton	Shepherdstown, Jefferson	FWS
Lohman, Pearl Ida	Sharpsburg, Md, Washington	F
Maddex, Margaret Banks	Shepherdstown, Jefferson	FWS
Mills, Marie	Sharpsburg, Md., Washington	WS
Moler, Naomi	Shepherdstown, Jefferson	FWS
Palmer, Clara Lutitia	Minnehaha Springs, Pocahontas	S
Poffenberger, Madge Elizabeth	Sharpsburg, Md., Washington	FWS
Pultz, Ada Mabel	Romney, Hampshire	S
Reinhart, Mary Locher	Shepherdstown, Jefferson	S
Roby, Dessie Alice	Maysville, Grant	S

Name	Post Office — County	Terms
Shobe, Leota	Petersburg, Grant	S
Trump, Fannie Marshall	Kearneysville, Jefferson	FWS
Vanscoy, Gladys Wilmoth	Kerens, Randolph	S
Williams, Eleanor Imogene	Martinsburg, Berkeley	FW
Bell, Cecil Porter	Shepherdstown, Jefferson	FWS
Billmyer, George Waters, Jr	Shepherdstown, Jefferson	FWS
Boyd, Woodford Lee	Charles Town, Jefferson	WS
Burns, Joseph C., Jr	Clintonville, Greenbrier	S
Denison, Lawrence	Shepherdstown, Jefferson	FWS
Hendricks, Allen Lemen	Shepherdstown, Jefferson	FWS
Knode, William Edgar	Shepherdstown (Md.), Wash	FWS
Koontz, Wilbur Ledru	Shepherdstown, Jefferson	FWS
Lowe, Charles Ashby	Shepherdstown, Jefferson	FWS
Miller, Harry Tanquaray	Gerrardstown, Berkeley	W
Miller, Jacob Harrison	Wardensville, Hardy	S
Mills, Anddrew Schamel	Sharpsburg, Md., Washington	FWS
Moler, Holland Kerfoot	Shepherdstown, Jefferson	FWS
Mose, James Frederick	Sharpsburg, Md., Washington	FWS
Reed, Thomas Godfrey	Needmore, Hardy	S
Rush, William Jacob	Shepherdstown, Jefferson	FS
Sites, Johnson	Upper Tract, Pendleton	F
Sperow, Charles Billmyer	Shepherdstown, Jefferson	FW
Walper, William	Shepherdstown, Jefferson	FWS
Wilkins, M. Allen	Rock Oak, Hardy	S

FRESHMEN

Name	Post Office — County	Terms
Arnold, Ethel Lee	Romney, Hampshire	WS
Billmyer, Edna Marshall	Shepherdstown, Jefferson	F
Bloom, Alta Elizabeth	Slanesville, Hampshire	S
Bloom, Beulah	Slanesville, Hampshire	S
Boswell, Mary Katherine	Shepherdstown, Jefferson	FWS
Davis, Cora Frances	Hanging Rock, Hampshire	S
Dickey, Millie Virginia	Levels, Hampshire	S
Didawick, Irene Virginia	Wardensville, Hardy	FWS
Feltner, Ella Louise	Martinsburg, Berkeley	FWS
Fleming, Thelma Lloyd	Kearneysville, Jefferson	FWS
Foltz, Annie Belle	Mathias, Hardy	S
Fultz, Estella Mary	Slanesville, Hampshire	F
Gantt, Nellie	Cherry Run, Morgan	W
Grapes, Edithe Frances	Pleasant Dale, Hampshire	S
Halterman, Lona Prudence	Mathias, Hardy	S
Harrell, Grace Anna	Shepherdstown, Jefferson	FWS
Hawse, Bessie Claire	Rock Oak, Hardy	S

Name	Post Office — County	Terms
Heare, Emma Edna	Rock Oak, Hardy	S
Hendricks, Mary Virginia	Shenandoah Junct'n, Jefferson	FWS
Henkle, Bessie Grove	Shenandoah Junct'n, Jefferson	FWS
Hill, Elizabeth Lee	Shepherdstown, Jefferson	F
Hollida, Virginia Beatrice	Martinsburg, Berkeley	FS
Hutton, Laura Virginia	Shepherdstown, Jefferson	FWS
Kern, Iva Sibyl	Capon Bridge, Hampshire	S
Kershner, Grace Darling	Henry, Grant	F
Knox, Virginia Victor	Shepherdstown, Jefferson	FWS
Lewis, Icy Agnes	Cacapehon, Hampshire	W
May, Lydia Gladys	Mathias, Hardy	FWS
Miller, Garnetta Virginia	Martinsburg, Berkeley	FWS
Miller, Geneva	Baker, Hardy	S
Moler, Martha Virginia	Shenandoah Junct'n, Jefferson	FWS
Myers, Florence Gertrude	Shepherdstown, Jefferson	FWS
Myers, Lillian Evelyn	Shenandoah Junct'n, Jefferson	FWS
Pine, Mary Blanche	Kearneysville, Jefferson	FWS
Shirley, Corinne Hightman	Shenandoah Junct'n, Jefferson	FWS
Slaughter, Delva Elizabeth	Shenandoah Junct'n, Jefferson	FWS
Stickel, Eva Bell	Wardensville, Hardy	FWS
Strieby, Alta Rachel	Shepherdstown, Jefferson	FWS
Strieby, Viola	Shepherdstown, Jefferson	FWS
Stump, Goldie	Slanesville, Hampshire	S
Swisher, Dollie Frances	Levels, Hampshire	S
Thompson, Mabel Leone	Shepherdstown, Jefferson	FWS
Unger, Margaret F.	Shepherdstown, Jefferson	FWS
White, Glayds Grace	Minnehaha Springs, Pocahontas	S
Bean, Orvon Ray	Fabius, Hardy	S
Boyd, E. McDaniel	Charles Town, Jefferson	F
Day, George Hamilton	Points, Hampshire	S
Engle, Jesse Aglionby	Shenandoah Junct'n, Jefferson	FWS
Engle, Jessie Ruthven	Shenandoah Junct'n, Jefferson	WS
Ferrell, Richard Keys	Shepherdstown, Jefferson	FWS
Folk, Adrian Irving	Martinsburg, Berkeley	FWS
Folk, Jacob Wintermoyers	Shepherdstown, Jefferson	FWS
Folk, Louis Reynolds	Martinsburg, Berkeley	FWS
Gochenour, John Chrisman	Baker, Hardy	WS
Grove, Thomas Pinkney	Shenandoah Junct'n, Jefferson	F
Hamstead, E. E.	Masontown, Preston	F
Jenkins, Daniel	Kearneysville, Jefferson	F
Louthan, Ross Ogden	Shepherdstown, Jefferson	FW
McDonald, Charles Lee	Shepherdstown, Jefferson	W
McDonald, George Hall	Shepherdstown, Jefferson	W
McKee, Newton Byers	Shepherdstown, Jefferson	FWS

Name	Post Office — County	Terms
McQuilkin, Franklin	Shepherdstown, Jefferson	FWS
Martin, Guy Ronald	Romney, Hampshire	WS
Melester, Harry Emmert	Shepherdstown, Jefferson	F
Miller, Edward Lester	Martinsburg, Berkeley	F
Miller, Harry Lentz	Shepherdstown, Jefferson	FW
Miller, Robert	Shepherdstown, Jefferson	F
Mullendore, Albertus Daniel	Trego, Md., Washington	FWS
Poffenberger, Owen	Points, Hampshire	W
Portmess, Dewey	Cacapehon, Hampshire	W
Power, Burr Wilson	Levels, Hampshire	W
Power, Francis Ray	Levels, Hampshire	S
Power, Joseph Rodney	Levels, Hampshire	S
Pownell, Edgar Brian	Romney, Hampshire	FW
Shipley, Elkins	Shepherdstown, Jefferson	S
Shipper, Bethuel Midelton	Martinsburg, Berkeley	FW
Snyder, William I	Wardensville, Hardy	S
Snyder, William Mayo	Shenandoah Junct'n, Jefferson	FW
Swisher, William Bernard	South Branch, Hampshire	F
Watson, Edgar B	Three Churches, Jefferson	S

STUDENTS IN SPECIAL SUBJECTS

Name	Post Office — County	Terms
Banks, Hetty Mildred	Shepherdstown, Jefferson	W
Denison, Magdalene	Shepherdstown, Jefferson	FW
Folk, Sara	Shepherdstown, Jefferson	FWS
Fulk, Nellie Bowen	Kearneysville, Jefferson	WS
Fulton, Dorothy Tucker	Cherry Run, Morgan	F
Kelsey, Ella M	Shepherdstown, Jefferson	F
Knott, Esther May	Shepherdstown, Jefferson	F
Louthan, Emma	Shepherdstown, Jefferson	S
Myers, Ruth Allan	Martinsburg, Berkeley	F
Worman, Ruth Magdalene	Shepherdstown, Jefferson	FWS
Tyson, Jesse Raymond	Berkeley Springs, Morgan	S

STUDENTS IN SUMMER SCHOOL, 1916

Name	Post Office	County
Banks, Hetty Mildred	Shepherdstown	Jefferson
Bell, Agnes Mae	Shepherdstown	Jefferson
Bell, Bessie Bonnylin	Bardane	Jefferson
Canfield, Virginia Pascal	Paw Paw	Morgan
Comer, Ola Virginia	Shenandoah Junction	Jefferson
Crosfield, Anna Hunt	Berkeley Springs	Morgan
Dailey, Frances Yates	Shepherdstown	Jefferson

Name	Post Office	County
Denison, Gertrude	Shepherdstown	Jefferson
Engle, Beulah Forester	Charles Town	Jefferson
Engle, Jessie Melvin	Charles Town	Jefferson
Feaster, Maude Ethel	Greenland	Grant
Fortney, Bethsheba Evelyn	Kingwood	Preston
Fuss, Neva Lucile	Hedgesville	Berkeley
Gates, Tracy E.	Cherry Run	Morgan
Hale, Kate Phipps	Rogersville, Tenn.	Hawkins
Henkle, Mary Virginia	Shenandoah Junction	Jefferson
Hiett, Lillie Pauline	Great Cacapon	Morgan
Hockmann, Ella Mabel	Slanesville	Hampshire
Hollida, Ethel Mae	Martinsburg	Berkeley
Hollida, Maude VanMetre	Martinsburg	Berkeley
Huffman, Grace	Berkeley Springs	Morgan
Kerns, Iva Sibyl	Capon Bridge	Hampshire
Knode, Martha	Shepherdstown	Jefferson
Lawson, Elsie	Manassas, Va.	Prince William
May, Ada Elizabeth	Mathias	Hardy
Mills, Louella Augusta	Sharpsburg, Md.	Washington
Mohler, Bruce Virginia	Martinsburg	Berkeley
Morgan, Augusta Jackson	Shepherdstown	Jefferson
Muldoon, Gertrude Virginia	Shepherdstown	Jefferson
Needy, Mary Catherine	Shepherdstown	Jefferson
Offutt, Edna Venora	Augusta	Hampshire
Payne, Grace Fleming	Hedgesville	Berkeley
Portmess, Fay Marie	Cacapehon	Hampshire
Rider, Elinor Virginia	Halltown	Jefferson
Selvey, Helen Rebecca	Shepherdstown	Jefferson
Strieby, Alta	Shepherdstown	Jefferson
Strieby, Carrie Lucille	Shepherdstown	Jefferson
Strieby, Viola Frances	Shepherdstown	Jefferson
Trump, Fannie Marshall	Kearneysville	Jefferson
VanMetre, Lillian Mae	Martinsburg	Berkeley
Walker, Lola Virginia	Shepherdstown	Jefferson
Wheaton, Vivian Elizabeth	Petersburg	Grant
Williams, Kathryn Folk	Shepherdstown	Jefferson
Williams, Nannie Louraine	Shepherdstown	Jefferson
Wolford, Eunice Lowell	Romney	Hampshire
Worman, Ruth Magdalene	Shepherdstown	Jefferson
Bell, Ellis Clifton	Bardane	Jefferson
Bell, Roy Austin	Shepherdstown	Jefferson
Burch, John C.	Fabius	Hardy
Butts, Thomas Reed	Hedgesville	Berkeley
Carter, Leroy Gray	Great Cacapon	Morgan

Name	Post Office	County
Engle, Kenneth Hendricks	Shenandoah Junction	Jefferson
Flaherty, Hubert Bertram	Shepherdstown	Jefferson
Harman, Robert Dove	Riverton	Pendleton
Hartzell, George	Shepherdstown	Jefferson
Hutton, Welton Brotherton	Shepherdstown	Jefferson
Keesecker, Palmer Thomas	Hedgesville	Berkeley
Kiser, William Raymond	Alaska	Mineral
Lemen, Wiloughby Morgan	Shepherdstown	Jefferson
Lord, Allen Phelps	Martinsburg	Berkeley
Lowry, Hubert David	Springdale	Fayette
McKee, Kirkland Shepherd	Shepherdstown	Jefferson
Mathias, Floyd Branson	Shepherdstown	Jefferson
Moyers, Grant Tyler	Mathias	Hardy
Nichols, Daniel Shirley	Harpers Ferry	Jefferson
Ours, Lester	Petersburg	Grant
Ropp, George William	Hedgesville	Berkeley
Scanlon, Wilko Gruver	Three Churches	Hampshire
Shanholtzer, James Clinton	Shepherdstown	Jefferson
Staubs, Earle William	Harpers Ferry	Jefferson
Triplett, Charles Clay	Shepherdstown	Jefferson
Watson, Jethro Scott	Three Churches	Hampshire
Wolford, Feaster	Dry Fork	Tucker
Worman, Charles Edwin	Shepherdstown	Jefferson

SUMMARY OF ENROLLMENT, 1916-1917

	Young Women	Young Men	Total
Seniors, Normal	11	6	17
Juniors, Normal	6	4	10
Seniors, Short Course	9	4	13
Seniors, Secondary	1	1	2
Juniors, Secondary	21	23	44
Sophomores	25	20	45
Freshmen	44	37	81
Students in Special Subjects	10	1	11
Summer School, 1916	46	28	74
	173	124	297
Deduct those counted twice	23	11	34
Total	150	113	263

COUNTIES REPRESENTED

Augusta, Va	2	Mineral	5
Berkeley	26	Montgomery, Md	1
Fayette	1	Morgan	13
Grant	8	Pendleton	3
Greenbrier	1	Pocahontas	2
Hampshire	34	Preston	5
Hardy	20	Prince William, Va	1
Hawkins, Tenn	1	Randolph	4
Jefferson	122	Tucker	3
Madison, Va	1	Washington, Md	10

BASEBALL TEAM

ATHLETIC FIELD

Total Enrollment

AND NUMBER OF GRADUATES SHEPHERD COLLEGE

	Number Enrolled	Number of Diplomas Issued	Number of Different Graduates
1874	145	21	21
1875	160	28	28
1876	136	27	27
1877	102	8	8
1878	94	11	11
1879	93	18	18
1880	55	14	14
1881	71	5	5
1882	58	9	9
1883	62	1	1
1884	59	9	9
1885	65	12	12
1886	65	3	3
1887	69	5	5
1888	64	3	3
1889	71	4	4
1890	69	3	3
1891	87	4	4
1892	90	7	7
1893	99	12	12
1894	91	8	8
1895	103	7	7
1896	103	16	12
1897	100	15	8
1898	88	8	5
1899	105	13	10
1900	116	20	13
1901	127	7	7
1902	151	12	10
1903	143	7	5
1904	153	12	11
1905	175	10	10
1906	158	7	6

	Number Enrolled	Number of Diplomas Issued	Number of Different Graduates
1907	200	11	9
1908	238	5	5
1909	276	21	20
1910	295	21	21
1911	303	46	44
1912	274	36	31
1913	268	39	39
1914	262	38	38
1915	240	33	33
1916	284	58	57
1917	263	32	32
	6,021	687	646

INDEX

Page

Announcements, 1917-1918...................................... 5

Art 26

Athletics 19

Boarding 12

Books 12

Buildings 13

Calendar 4

Commencement Week, 1917.................................... 5

Commercial Subjects.. 28

Conditions of Admission.................................... 10

Correspondence Study....................................... 25

Courses of Study Outlined.................................. 21

Credit for Work Done Elsewhere............................. 10

Dormitory, The... 16

Education 28

English 34

Enrollment of Students..................................... 48

Enrollment, Summary of..................................... 55

Expenses 11

Expression 36

Faculty 5

French 36

German 37

Gymnasium 15

History of Shepherd College................................ 8

History 38

Home Economics... 40

Laboratories 13

Latin 41

Library 15

Literary Societies.. 16

Location of Shepherd College................................. 8

Manual Training... 42

Mathematics 42

Music 44

Official Boards... 3

Orchestra, Shepherd College.................................. 19

Publications, Student... 19

Review Courses, Teachers..................................... 24

Science .... 44.

Short Course.. 21

Summer School....:.............................. 25

Tuition 11

Y. W. C. A. and Y. M. C. A.................................... 18

Lightning Source UK Ltd.
Milton Keynes UK
UKHW010905231118
332790UK00007B/229/P